UNDERSTANDING ZEN

UNDERSTANDING ZEN

Benjamin Radcliff
Amy Radcliff

Charles E. Tuttle Company, Inc.
Boston • Rutland, Vermont • Tokyo

First published in the United States in 1993 by
the Charles E. Tuttle Company, Inc. of Rutland, Vermont
& Tokyo, Japan, with editorial offices at
77 Central Street, Boston, Massachusetts 02109.

Library of Congress Cataloging-in-Publication Data

Radcliff, Benjamin, 1963-
    Understanding Zen / Benjamin Radcliff, Amy Radcliff.
       p. cm.
    Includes bibliographical references.
    ISBN 0-8048-1808-8 (pbk. : acid-free paper)
    1. Zen Buddhism—Doctrines—Introductions. I. Radcliff, Amy,
1960- . II. Title.
BQ9268.5.R33 1993
294.3'927—dc20   92-42624
                                                CIP

Cover design by Lisa Diercks

PRINTED IN THE UNITED STATES

CONTENTS

PREFACE
The Logic of Zen

There are occasions and causes why and wherefore in all things.

—William Shakespeare

Logical consequences are the scarecrows of fools and the beacons of wise men.

—T.H. Huxley

As rational animals, human beings attempt to understand their lives. Unfortunately, science, logic, and our own experience all seem to suggest that life is devoid of any final significance, purpose, or meaning. We seem to be nothing more than short-lived accidents of evolution, born only to die. The unsettling reality is thus that the same capacity for reason which allows us to question and examine our lives also illustrates the ultimate futility and transitoriness of our existence. The problem of life, in short, is that life does not make sense.

The human fascination with mystical or religious experience, and systems such as Zen which are thought to promise or embody it, is a direct result of this existential anxiety, for if life is to have meaning, it is clear that such meaning can be found only in a qualitatively different sort of experience than that to which we are accustomed. Unfortunately, precisely because the mystical transcends the conventional, it is logically impossible to describe it in terms of symbolic systems (such as language) which, by definition, are conventional. "Explaining" Zen is thus very much like telling the blind about sight: ultimately it cannot be done, for the obvious reason that sight cannot be reduced to—i.e., it transcends—the remaining four senses. The literature on mysticism in general, and Zen in particular, thus tends to be quite vague, in that we of necessity lack the tools to discuss the subject in a meaningful fashion.

Happily, though, we can examine both the logic of the road that leads to mystical experience and the consequences of that experience. In other words, while we cannot provide an adequate account of Zen when confined by language, we can explicate what we call, for lack of a better term, "the logic of Zen." By this we mean the process of rational argument through which the human mind can make the intuitive leap to Zen.

It is thus our view that Zen and rationality are complementary, rather than opposed, such that one implies the other. The task is to make use of the latter so as to open the doors to the former. We hope that such a strategy will prove more accessible and reader-friendly than the more impressionistic and elliptical approach associated with the traditional literature.

We owe a considerable debt to the many people who have influenced our thinking on these matters. While all cannot be listed here, we particularly acknowledge the work of Masao Abe, Fritjof Capra, Douglas Hofstadter, C.G. Hempel, Hermann Hesse, Robert Heilbroner, David Hume, Thomas Kuhn, Imre Lakatos, Karl Marx, Karl Popper, Pierre-Joseph Proudhon, Arthur Schopenhauer, D.T. Suzuki, and Alan Watts. We are grateful to Pat Aylward, Gerry Berk, Paul Gabel, Gretchen Hower, Tom Lavrakas, Alex Pacek, Paul Pudaite, and Greg Romano for reading portions of previous drafts. Our thanks to Chad Wishchuk for preparing the index. Thanks also to everyone at Tuttle for their support and encouragement throughout the development of this project.

Benjamin Radcliff
Amy Radcliff
London, 20 May 1992

For Linda Caise and Anne Gille,
and
for the memory of Kenneth Gille and Mildred Mosier

CHAPTER ONE
Approach to Zen

Truth is a pathless land.
　　　　　—Krishnamurti

Enlightenment does not care how you get there.
　　　　　—Thaddeus Golas

The Zen establishment makes a great deal of noise about the universality of Zen, but remains notoriously provincial when the dictum is taken seriously. While there is surely some pluralism within that establishment, it is nonetheless a relatively self-contained universe mired in dogma, ritual, and tradition. Unfortunately, such parochialism has made most accounts of Zen virtually incomprehensible to the Western reader. The present study is an attempt to make Zen more accessible by stripping away the layers of orthodoxy that have come to surround it. We will present Zen as a secular doctrine without any necessary relationship to Buddhism or Eastern culture.

In recent decades attempts to distance Zen from its Buddhist foundations have been assailed as "deviations" that threaten the integrity of Zen itself. At an abstract, theoretical level, it may in fact be impossible to remove Zen entirely from Buddhism, since the experience associated with Zen is (as we detail in chapter five) arguably a Buddhist one. The issue is trivial, though, in that it is devoid of any practical relevance. One need neither become a Buddhist nor even be familiar with Buddhism to experience and appreciate Zen. While theoreticians may argue with themselves over the relationship between Zen and Buddhism, such disputes are modern manifestations of scholastic quibbling about how many angels can fit on the head of the ecclesiastical pin. While Buddhism is a religion, Zen surely is not.

The hostility toward an accessible, secular Zen is in large part a reaction to the "popularization" of Zen introduced by the Beats, Alan Watts, and (in the view of some) even D.T. Suzuki. The establishment has apparently come to believe that intellectual accounts of the subject nourish a kind of pseudo-Zen the depends upon the very mental processes that the student of Zen seeks to avoid. The result has been a reactionary retreat into an elitist keeper-of-the-faith mentality which views Zen as a terribly solemn and tedious endeavor available only to those willing to devote themselves to traditional study with traditional Nipponese methods. Such a judgement is a lamentable perversion of the spirit of Zen. We believe it possible to explicitly and directly "explain" the road to Zen in conventional, everyday language, in a manner that will be understandable to any intelligent, curious reader.

Such a project need not produce a watered down version of Zen. There is nothing inherent in the subject that requires that depth be sacrificed for the sake of approachability. The tension is not between a readable treatment of Zen and a rigorous one; it is between an accessible one and a purposefully exclusionary one.

The seeds of the exclusionary nature of contemporary Zen are to be found in the nature of the subject itself. Given that the study of Zen is the study of the structure and meaning of human experience, given that it is an endeavor that has, as its end, a genuine understanding of both ourselves and the universe of which we are a part, the subject certainly *seems* abstruse. Even among Zen adherents who should know better, there is a tendency to view Zen as dreadfully profound and arcane—the philosophical equivalent to high energy physics. Thus, the notion that the ordinary person can fathom Zen becomes as ludicrous as the suggestion that the average individual, untutored in advanced mathematics and theoretical physics, can fully understand quantum mechanics or the General Theory of Relativity. If we are to

4

believe the dominant voices in the Zen community, you can only study Zen in the way you would study physics—by long, arduous, disciplined effort under the tutelage of those who already know the way. Of course, just as few of us have the time or disposition to pursue a graduate degree in physics, few of us have the inclination to study Zen formally under the guidance of a Master.

The nature of the traditional approach to instruction is well illustrated by the following all too typical episode. While giving a talk to a group of psychoanalysts, a Zen Master responded to the question "What is Zen?" by peeling and consuming a banana. An observer, understandably perplexed, asked if the instructor could possibly elaborate. The instructor did so by smashing the banana into the questioner's face. After the audience continued to press for a more intelligible answer, the Master finally replied that "Zen is an elephant copulating with a flea."[1]

There are two possible reactions to this sort of experience. The first is to assume that Zen is so "profound" that this nonsensical answer is actually appropriate. Despite, or, because of, the inanity of the reply, we are led to believe that there is something very "deep" going on. To be sure, we have no clue as to the nature of this profundity, but we are sure that it is there. A second and less charitable conclusion is that the Master is purposely misleading and confusing his audience. The latter would appear more likely.

The general justification for the refusal or inability of establishment Zen to express itself in ways that are easily accessible to the Western reader is that a central aspect of Zen is (as we shall see) the transcendence of all words and concepts. Indeed, the experience that is Zen consists entirely of transcending or "moving beyond" all conventional ideas, concepts, and words. Because Zen is not about words or the concepts they represent, it is inconceivable that you could use these things to explain it. Given that Zen is predicated upon the opposition to all theoretical or abstract notions, it seems ridiculous to attempt to describe it in such terms. In essence, to produce a set of philosophical propositions that are alleged to "explain" Zen is logically inconsistent with the premises of Zen. To engage in this type of philosophical analysis, it is said, is to miss the point entirely.

Thus proponents of Zen have generally argued that any attempt to discuss the subject must be indirect and suggestive, rather than explicit and analytic. One thus describes Zen in much the same way that one draws a three dimensional object—a cube, say—in the two dimensions of a blackboard: by producing the shadow that the transcendental object throws in the conventional world. A cube transcends the conceptual map of a two-dimensional world, just as the experience of Zen transcends the world of concepts and ideas. Zen literature thus "hints" rather than "tells," because telling is impossible. The result is that the literature is no more Zen than the blackboard etching is a cube. Both the drawing and the words are poor intimations, i.e., hints, about the things to which they refer. While such hints may be the best that can be accomplished, it leaves us with the impression that Zen is like grace—it's there in the ether waiting to be found, but no one can tell us how to find it.

The attitude that a discussion of Zen must be indirect is midwife to the enigmatic nature of much Zen instruction. To take a typical example, a student asks a *roshi* (a master "certified" to "teach" Zen) why it is that "Zen masters don't bother to explain things." After some exchanges in which the *roshi* repeatedly declines to explain why masters will not explain, the student is told "Zen is not for you."[2]

Those whose sympathies lie with the questioner rather than the *roshi* are unlikely to be pleased with another Zen staple known as the *koan*. One of the principal forms of instruction in (Rinzai) Zen, the *koan*, or problem, contains some important insight which the student is to discover. One of the best known is the question "What is the sound of one hand clapping?" Clearly, the question is absurd, in

6

that, as the proverb suggests, "It takes two hands to clap." In the absence of any obvious answer, the student looks for "deeper" or symbolic meanings, but there are none to be found. The *koan* is thus like the demand for a description of a four-sided triangle. The explicit purpose is to confuse and frustrate until, in desperation, one is forced to abandon all conceptual thinking. When finally taken to such a point, one has "solved" the *koan* by learning to let go of the artificial and restraining framework of conventional thought.

Thus, one traditionally studies Zen through a laborious process of torturing the rational mind until it surrenders. This practice and similarly protracted periods of sitting meditation (*zazen*) form the foundation of Zen training. While there has been much sound and fury about the necessity for not merely transplanting this decidedly Japanese system into the Western world, most attempts to create a distinctively American vision of Zen instruction have amounted to little more than modifying the Japanese approach to fit the timbre of American life. Rather than reconsider the entire monastic approach, revisionists have concentrated on merely refining it to meet the contingencies of contemporary culture. The Zen establishment continues to cling to the notion that without protracted formal training on the Japanese model, replete with a *roshi*-student relationship, one is virtually incapable of becoming enlightened. Accordingly, any attempt to "study" Zen intellectually, without the discipline of established method, is doomed to outright failure, or worse, a psychological attachment to a *faux* Zen. To those trained in the Nipponese tradition, "mastering" Zen requires tremendous dedication, long study, and subservience to authority. Enlightenment, the argument declaims, can only be obtained through devotion and single-mindedness of purpose. Ideally, it is pursued through full time monastic instruction; failing that, it must be approached with an "outpatient" program.

We find such a view elitist, inappropriate to American culture, and contrary to the spirit of Zen. We agree instead with the admonition of the monk Dogen that you don't need monasteries or teachers—that enlightenment is something that is in reach of everyone, all the time. In sum, enlightenment is a process that you can begin right this minute, without the aid of a *roshi*, monasticism, asceticism, or what Charlotte Joko Beck aptly calls the "agonizing despair" of protracted *zazen*. This book takes the unfashionable position that while Zen is profound in its own way, it is not so complex or esoteric that it cannot be studied and experienced outside of a student-teacher relationship. Zen is a part of the human condition. Its realization does not depend upon a Master, a guru, or any particular method.

Such an approach is radically opposed to the current vogue in Zen literature. Our purpose is to do exactly what others have alleged cannot be done: to offer a clear, precise, and rational description of Zen. Although it is, in a literal sense, thoroughly impossible to express or understand Zen conceptually, it is quite possible to convey a significant amount of what Zen "is about" not only in conventional language but in a straightforward fashion. While the content of the "experience" that is the final point of Zen does indeed lay beyond the world of language and concepts, one can explain, in some detail, the logic that leads to that experience and the implications that follow from it. Thus the point is not to portray Zen in rational terms, but rather to point the way toward Zen in a rational and understandable way.

The program of *koan* and meditation has the same end, though it relies upon a different method. In both cases the purpose is to lead the student to what he or she cannot be taught. The difference is that the traditional method functions negatively, by putting barriers in the acolyte's path. Instead, we pursue the same goal with different means. Rather than the route of frustration and obstruction, we choose the more direct, less painful path of encouragement and explication. The standard approach relies on the stick; we choose the carrot.

We begin with the realization that while Zen is beyond logic (because it is beyond all concepts) it is not the case that Zen is an illogical hodgepodge of pseudo-mystical nonsense. To transcend logic is not to be illogical. Rather, it is to see in such a way that logic is no longer necessarily useful. The path toward that understanding may itself be quite orderly and logical. In much the same way, one may logically describe an experience or an activity that may help one to reach the experience or learn how to perform the activity. To use an obvious example, one might learn to skydive in terms of concepts and theories, but to jump is immediately to transcend all the words and ideas about it. What we hope to provide is a conceptual, logical map that points the way toward transcending all concepts and all logic—in other words, toward Zen.

Again, by pursuing such a method, we are departing from Zen tradition. However, this tradition is itself just another set of concepts. Indeed, from the perspective of Zen, the entire tradition is just more mental clutter. We thus face the first—and perhaps most endearing—Zen paradox: one can abandon the whole of Zen tradition, and still remain within that tradition precisely for doing so.

Still, purists may protest that we are engaging in an anomaly. How, they might say, can we hope to transcend the limits of the intellect by clutching at it? What they fail to see is that any attempt to transcend ordinary consciousness must necessarily begin with that consciousness and offer a method for moving beyond it. The *koan* is certainly one such method. One strives and struggles to solve the puzzle, until one not only sees but feels that there is no solution—that the problem lies in one's thinking rather than in the *koan* itself. The *koan* is thus a method whereby one uses conventional thinking to recognize the limitations of such a way of thinking. What we propose follows a similar logic. We begin with ordinary consciousness and proceed to show, through conventional reasoning, why it is insufficient. Both approaches result in the same end—that is, in Zen.

We do not pretend that an individual can become enlightened by reading a book. The difficulty of the struggle to escape the prison of dualistic thinking cannot be avoided. We do not propose any easy solutions; insights do not come freeze-dried or microwave-ready. Instead, we merely suggest that considerable progress in the quest for enlightenment can be made in a relatively painless way when one encourages, rather than frustrates, the mind.

In much the same vein, we also reject the romantic view that Zen is a celebration of irrationality that has survived by appealing to would-be mystics who are disaffected with our rationalist culture. On the contrary, we argue that Zen has a special appeal to individuals who seek but are unable to find answers that conform to the dictates of reason and experience, for those who do not believe in spirits and angels for the same reason that they do not believe in Santa Claus, and for those who do not believe that there are easy answers to the difficult problems of life. Zen provides an answer by denying that answers are necessary or possible, by denying that any philosophy or religion can be an adequate description of reality.[3] Further, this conclusion applies to Zen as well, so that in coming to "understand" Zen, one learns, above all, to leave it behind.

In other words, the end of what we might call the "research project" of Zen—the attempt to experience Zen—is itself beyond Zen. This point is an important one, in that it affects the coherence of the method we utilize to "explain" Zen. As said before, it is impossible to express Zen in terms of language. This point was illustrated by referring to Zen as an "experience" whose content can only be understood by having it rather than discussing it. However, in a strict sense, to say that Zen is an experience is also incorrect, for reasons that will become clear in the following chapter. This example illustrates the general problem of attempting to "explain" Zen, in that it simply cannot be done. One says that "Zen is an experience" but then is forced to admit that Zen is emphatically not an experience. This is quite confusing and is one of the reasons that the standard approach eschews explanation.

The way out of the dilemma is to realize that we can make provisional statements not about what Zen *is*, but what Zen *is like*. We begin by making statements that are strictly wrong, but which are as close as we can come. By tentatively accepting such propositions, we climb a ladder of half truths, but once we reach the top, we can look back and see the various rungs that led us there for what they are. Thus we will engage in making positive statements about Zen, not because such statements are absolutely true, but because it is useful to do so—because they form a basis of understanding that will ultimately illustrate the greater truth of which they are merely poor reflections. In the process they will expose their own shortcomings as descriptions of Zen. In this way, we might begin by saying "Zen is an experience" but, as we progress up the ladder of understanding, we will come to see how and why Zen is not experience.

II

To anticipate what follows, we will argue that the first step on the path toward Zen is contained in the following rather unremarkable proposition:

> There is a distinction, on the one hand, between ideas, concepts, and symbols, and on the other hand, the actual things to which those ideas, concepts, and symbols refer.

On its face, it is difficult to see how such a truism could form the basis for an insight into the fundamental texture of reality. Surely, it is apparent that the word "tree" is distinct from the large, leafy plant to which the word refers. Similarly, the concept of the tree as a general notion by which we categorize objects is just a mental construct; it is not equivalent to actual empirical trees.

Despite the obviousness of this fact, it is one that we constantly fail to see. In large part, Zen consists of coming to see—that is, to experience—the truth of this observation in a way that is vivid, immediate, and personal. Radical changes in the way we view the world and ourselves follow from taking seriously the thoroughly non-obvious implications of this realization.

NOTES

1. Philip Kapleau, *Zen: Dawn in the West* (Boston: Beacon Press, 1982).
2. Kapleau, *Zen: Dawn in the West.*
3. Both religion and philosophy remain "other-worldly," i.e., they attempt to solve the problem of life by referring to elements external to life. The former suggests that salvation is possible in the form of eventual migration to another, better, and unknowable world. Philosophy relies upon theories which explain away the chaos of reality. In this way, both ultimately require a literal or figural leap of faith. The former requires that one accept that there is another existence beyond that implied by our experience. The latter asks that we assume that reality can be reduced to concepts and abstractions—that life can be reduced to something else. Zen asks you to assume nothing, to believe nothing, to accept nothing on faith. Instead of postulating a world beyond death that is superior to the world of experience, or a world of words and symbols that is inferior to the waking world, Zen focuses solely on the sensory world. By so doing it offers a direct and immediate answer that is in terms of life itself.

CHAPTER TWO
The Caverns of Reason

No truth is more certain, more independent of all others, and less in need of proof than this: that all that exists for knowledge, and therefore this whole world, is only object in relation to subject, perception of a perceiver, in a word, idea.

—Arthur Schopenhauer

What is interesting about logical thought . . . is that once having been mastered, its rules master us.

—Robert Heilbroner

The human mind is the most versatile and powerful tool yet devised. Still, the mind, like all human characteristics, evolved through interaction with the environment, in accordance with the principle of natural selection. Hence, we have large brains and highly complex minds for precisely the same reason we have opposable thumbs: because they are useful.

In the quest for survival, we have learned to think. We have gained greater and greater ability to understand and manipulate the world by fitting its contours to the dictates of abstract reason. While this peculiar ability has proven extraordinarily valuable, it has also introduced certain problems. Though we gain immeasurably from our capacity to reason, we also tend to become unknowingly ensnared within an existential maze of our own devising.

From the perspective of Zen, the human predicament results from the fact that we have done just that. We have become trapped within the walls of reason, wandering through tunnels that lead nowhere but to death. As we shall see, this existential labyrinth is built with bricks of the mind. To free ourselves, we must first understand the nature of the prison. This in turn requires an appraisal of the logic of abstract thinking.

II

The explicit emphasis on abstractions in Western philosophy goes back at least to Plato. It is perhaps best exemplified by his "allegory of the cave." In this extended metaphor,

17

Plato posits a group of men imprisoned beneath earth. They are so confined that they are forced to look only straight ahead, where they see various shapes projected upon the wall. Unable to turn about, they do not see that these objects are merely shadows that are being reflected upon the wall. The "true" objects are being passed before a source of illumination which is located above and behind them and thus removed from their sight. Unaware of the deception, the hapless prisoners confuse these shadows as the objects themselves.

The plight of mankind, Plato suggests, is analogous. In our day to day lives, we see only the shadows of reality, the pale and incomplete reflections of a decidedly greater world. The objects of ordinary consciousness—trees, say—are only imperfect manifestations of the general idea, the "Form" in Plato's terms, of what we might call "treeness." Actual empirical trees, trees that you can touch, see, and otherwise directly experience, are real only in the same way that the flickering images upon the cave wall are real. Both are ephemeral illusions that distort our view of reality. An enlightened person, Plato suggests, recognizes this fact. He or she learns to see beyond particular trees to the Form or idea of tree.

This is precisely what is meant by an abstraction. Particulars are replaced by a notion of the general category to which the particulars are examples. Hence, large, woody plants with leaves cease being unique objects, becoming instead trees. In the same way, *The Merchant of Venice*, *Waiting for Godot*, and *Glengarry, Glen Ross* become "plays," Britain, France, and Spain "countries," hydrogen, helium, and lithium "elements," and so on.

Abstractions are wonderful examples of the even more general notion of a "concept." All concepts are themselves abstractions, but some, like logic, are abstractions of abstractions. In other words, we have an idea of treeness, but for it to be of any use, we must have other ideas, other abstractions, that delimit ideas and relate them. We need these second-order abstractions to make sense of the first-order abstractions. For example, if treeness is to be of any value, if it is to be a real abstraction, we must also have the rule that there are some things that are not trees.

In so doing, we have stumbled upon the idea—the meta-concept, if you will—of dualism. Simply put, all concepts are ultimately dichotomies. Either something is a tree or it is not. If a concept is not dualistic, it is vacuous, in that it does not differentiate. The purpose of abstraction is to have one set of objects which share some defining characteristics but not others. Hence, if some things cannot be placed within the abstraction and others outside of it, it is not really an abstraction. A concept that does not discriminate—which is not dual—is meaningless. Defining such a concept is a logical contradiction; it cannot be done. Ultimately, everything can be thought of as an analogue to binary numbers—either it is 1 or 0. To continue this analogy, you cannot have a number system that has only one value.

Thus, all abstractions make sense only if they can be compared to opposable terms. "Easy" is meaningless without "difficult," just as "up" makes no sense unless we can contrast it with "down." Even extremely general concepts such as "thing" are dualistic, in that they can be opposed to "nothing." Ideas that do not have immediately identifiable opposites, such as "chair," still have an opposing concept, in this case "not-chair," for the obvious reason that "chair" means nothing unless there are things which are not chairs.

The simplest conceptual scheme is one that consists of only one (necessarily dualistic) abstraction, say "self" and "not-self." In this scenario, there is only the self and everything else. The external world, the not-self, is an undifferentiated, uniform mass. The utility of this scheme is relatively small, and is quickly replaced with a more elaborate system that begins to draw distinctions between external and internal elements. The not-self is divided into trees, rivers, weather, and so on. Similarly, self becomes divided into, say, mind and body. Next, we might make further refinements, separating trees into "spruce," "sycamore," "elm," and so on, and perhaps mind into "conscious" and "unconscious" or even "id," "ego," and "superego." We also begin to develop higher order abstractions, such as "causality" and "time." As we increase the complexity of our conceptual framework, we gain a greater ability to comprehend, control, and predict our lives. In the greatest sense of the term, "science" means the totality of human efforts to do just that—to understand and manipulate the world. Hence, science is the process of building increasingly better sets of abstractions.

The popular view of science is mistaken in its implicit faith that concepts somehow exist in reality and are "discovered" by human cleverness. Instead, concepts are "built" or improvised as part of the scientific enterprise.

Concepts are devised by human beings; they are not inherent in the nature of the universe. Put another way, all concepts, all abstractions, are human artifacts. They represent our attempt to impose a structure on reality so as to achieve certain desired ends. To borrow an example normally attributed to Schopenhauer, we see the world as causally determined, because this allows us to intervene in nature to produce (or prevent) certain effects. In other words, we divide the world into causes and effects because doing so is a highly efficient means to the end of gratifying our desires.

These abstractions are created by and exist only in the human mind. By their very nature, abstractions and concepts are of our own devising. We use them as an interface between our selves and the world. They are a form of mental "technology," in that they are not a part of nature but a human creation. Of course, technology—say, the computer being used to write this book—is not waiting to be "discovered"; it is manufactured by human beings. Concepts are a

20

special type of technology, though, in that they are imaginary, i.e., we create them, but only mentally rather than physically. To belabor the point, concepts are tools of the human mind that translate sensory data into more usable forms. Data are thus processed, sorted, and reduced to more manageable proportions.

However, in processing the information, its "true" nature is (by definition) necessarily distorted. To use an analogy, suppose that, rather than seeing the world directly, you were only allowed to view images translated by camera onto a poor resolution video monitor such that the world looked much like a cubist painting. Everything would appear to consist of relatively large squares of equal size. There would be no rounded corners, no curves, no circles. Of course, reality would only appear to be so because the screen imposes an artificial structure on a much more complex reality. The screen produces an image of reality based upon its own internal capacities. In the same way, our concepts produce an image of the world predicated upon their structure. Differentiating the world into things and not-things is a function of our minds rather than the universe just as a world of equal squares is a function of the resolution of the screen rather than the world itself.

Given that conceptual systems are determined more or less collectively, it must be granted that our particular concepts are merely convention. As such they are arbitrary. For example, we use the convention "book" for the same set of objects that are denoted *das Buch* in another conventional system. Of course, this arbitrariness extends beyond linguistic notation, in that there are no objectively meaningful ways to discriminate. As a consequence, we rely upon agreements—conventions—about how to divide the world. Why, for example, are headaches—or colors for that matter—things rather than events?

Further, these conventions have no reality, in that by definition they are simply abstractions—things that exist only as ideas or images in our minds. I can imagine, i.e., I can generate, the idea of a satellite of this planet made entirely of green cheese; while the idea exists within my mind, the thing itself does not exist. In the same way, there is no such thing as "treeness" outside of my mind. In concrete reality, there are only individual trees.

The importance of this fact cannot be overstated. It casts into relativistic oblivion our most fundamental notions about the world. Time and causality, for example, are nothing but higher order abstractions. So too is the differentiation of the world into a set of discrete categories. Accordingly, these things simply do not exist. They are merely mental constructs, useful to imagine but with no independent reality.

For instance, we impose a structure called longitude and latitude on the geography of the world. This structure allows us to locate particular places, draw international borders, and move about the planet with comparative ease. Yet, surely neither latitude nor longitude really exist. When you cross the international dateline or the Tropic of Capricorn, you do not observe a pencil-thin line running from both horizons. As we all recognize, latitude and longitude are imaginary. They impose a strict and well defined Cartesian order on the surface of a planet where no such order exists. We posit this order, not because we think it actually exists, but because it helps us achieve certain desired ends.

In effect, this imposition of order upon chaos is the function of all concepts. We employ abstractions not because they are true, but because they help us solve problems. The division of the world into discrete objects, the differentiation of cause and effect, and all other conceptual notions are strictly analogous to longitude and latitude. They are fabrications produced by the human mind in an attempt to reduce complex reality to manageable form.

From the perspective of what is called the "philosophy of science"—the study of how human inquiry is best undertaken—it is quite uncontroversial to suggest that concepts are arbitrary constructions of the human mind. Science, taken again in the larger sense of all attempts to understand the world, is predicated not upon the accumulation of facts but on the building of better theories. Theories are merely sets of concepts, related by other (meta-) concepts such as logic. In this usage, theories are not merely speculations that are to be proved true or false. They are instead simplified explanations for some aspect of reality. As such, they are neither true nor false. They are simply more or less useful.

Hence, when Einstein suggested that $E = MC^2$, he was not implying that this relation is somehow real, but rather that it helps us understand the relationship between various concepts. Neither the concepts themselves (energy, mass, the speed of light) nor the mathematical operators relating them are part of the universe. It may well be that eventually another set of concepts related by higher order concepts, will be judged better—that is, more useful—than relativity in the same way that relativity replaced Newtonian physics. Ultimately, neither system is a part of the universe, but only a part of the human attempt to understand it.

This, of course, is the fundamental conclusion to be drawn from the theory of relativity. Space and time (and thus events "contained" within this system) are all relative to every particular observer, such that these ideas assume meaning only in the context of some observer's description of experience.[1] Contrary to common sense, the Newtonian interpretation of space and time as fixed entities is incorrect: time and space are in fact entirely relative to a perceiver. The point is simply that the seemingly self-evident and entirely obvious world of absolute time and space—the very foundation upon which consensus reality is constructed—is an arbitrary construct that we know to be patently false. We continue to cling to it in spite of its falsity for the very good reason that for most of us, most of the time, it makes practical sense to assume a Newtonian universe.

In much the same way, we believe that there is a strict law of cause and effect. From the perspective of the philosophy of science, though, the cause and effect linkage is only another convenient construction of the mind. It is assumed because it suits our purposes to do so. This is most readily seen at the subatomic level, where various particles gleefully defy the "law" of cause and effect.[2] Electrons, for example, appear to move without cause. In the wake of Heisenberg's now famous Uncertainty Principle, the general interpretation of quantum mechanics is that causality simply does not obtain at the atomic level. The prevailing view is not that there are (or even could be) causes that we are simply unable to discover with the present state of theory and technology, but rather that it is logically impossible that any appropriate causal law could exist. To repeat, the implication is that far from being a necessary part of reality, causation is only an attribute of the human mind's efforts to understand reality. Like all abstractions, causality proves itself useful in some situations but not in others.

This problem can be generalized to all our fundamental assumptions about reality. The most basic of these is Aristotle's principle of non-contradiction: a proposition cannot be both true and not-true, or, more generally, a thing cannot be simultaneously both a member of a given set and not a member of this set. As we have seen, non-contradiction is a second-order abstraction necessary to make all other abstractions meaningful. As normally understood, all conceptualization requires non-contradiction; without it, all rational discourse collapses. Put differently, our conceptual map of the world—even granting that it is different from the world—depends upon concepts being useful. If we eliminate non-contradiction, our concepts evaporate into nothingness.[3]

Unfortunately, non-contradiction does not uniformly obtain. The principle is violated with alarming regularity—a situation called antinomy. In the so-called "liar's paradox," for example, one says "I am lying." The paradox arises when we attempt to determine the truth value of the sentence, in that it is both true and false. Accordingly, the original sentence, while perfectly legitimate in its own terms, clearly violates the core and center of all reason.

Another paradox, offered by Bertrand Russell, touches upon set theory directly. There are two types of possible sets: (1) those that contain themselves as members, and (2) those that do not. An example of (2) is books about Zen, in that the set of all books about Zen is not itself a book about Zen. An example of (1) would be everything but books about Zen, in that the set of all things except Zen books is itself not a book about Zen. Russell asks that we imagine the set of all type (2) sets, i.e., the set of all sets that do not contain themselves as members. As the reader may verify by pondering this situation for a moment, this set is both type (2) and not type (2).

Despite the fact that even such basic notions as causality and non-contradiction are necessarily arbitrary, it is sometimes suggested that we might be able to devise systems that are so complex and refined that they adequately capture the totality of the universe. While strictly arbitrary—indeed, strictly wrong—such systems would be the ultimate vindication of science, in that they would reduce the world to a set of abstractions. In loosely Platonic terms, we would have discovered a (though not necessarily *the*) set of forms that drive reality. Such a set would not be well behaved, in that it would contain internal contradictions, given the violations of logic that would occur, but it would be enormously useful nonetheless. To borrow a phrase from economic science, the universe would behave "as if" it followed our system of concepts. In this way, we would have truly and finally come to "understand" the cosmos.

Implicit in Zen is the view that such a program is impossible, that the universe cannot be appreciated through concepts. Logically, this statement is so broad that it is almost non-falsifiable, meaning that we cannot assess its truth value.[4] Logicians rightly dismiss such statements as meaningless. However, it is possible to pose a "smaller," more concrete question that is not only amenable to logical inquiry but which also has in fact been rigorously investigated by the mathematician Kurt Godel.[5]

Simplifying somewhat, Godel has demonstrated that no closed axiomatic system—no set of concepts, in effect—can represent the full complexity of the properties of that system. In the terms of number theory in which Godel's Theorem was cast, no set of axioms about whole numbers can represent all true statements about such numbers. Put another way, our conceptual framework concerning whole numbers is "incomplete." There are things about whole numbers (i.e., the concept of whole numbers) which our concepts do not allow us to appreciate.

It is important to note that Godel's result applies to the internal structure of any set of theoretical propositions. It shows that even if we limit our attention to the world as described by our set of concepts (as opposed to the actual world of experience), these concepts cannot describe this "world," i.e., they cannot describe themselves! Hence, we need not commit ourselves to the view that there is more to the world than our concepts capture to understand that concepts cannot even capture their own limited world. We can take abstractions as givens, thus begging the fundamental questions raised above, and still come to the conclusion that abstractions cannot paint a "true" picture of reality.

III

The above discussion is by no means an indictment of abstract thought. Abstractions fuel the engine of reason. It is no exaggeration to suggest that it is the ability to engage in abstract reasoning that makes us distinctively human. Concepts are necessary for language, literature, agriculture, architecture, science, and technology—for civilization itself. The suggestion is not that there is anything wrong with abstractions, but only that we must not confuse them with reality.

The problem is that we consistently mistake abstractions for things that actually exist. In erecting an imaginary, clockwork, conceptual universe we have unwittingly allowed ourselves to become trapped within it.

As was previously suggested, the road to Zen begins with the realization that

> There is a distinction, on the one hand, between ideas, concepts, and symbols, and on the other, the actual things to which those ideas, concepts, and symbols refer.

In other words, we continuously confuse ideas about reality with reality itself. Our concepts are surely about reality, but they are not themselves real. We have created abstractions (say, the general idea of treeness) that represent other particular, existing things (trees), yet it is only the latter that actually exist. By carrying this process to its extreme, we have trapped ourselves within our minds, unable to experience anything but the idea of the tree.

Liters and gallons, for example, are abstractions representing fixed quantities of volume. There are no such things as liters or gallons. Instead, there are liters or gallons of something, and it is the somethings rather than the units of volume that are real. Of course, it is often convenient to be able to measure out exact amounts of these somethings, and so long as we do not confuse the unit of measurement with what is being measured, we benefit from our cleverness in developing such useful ideas. Imagine what would happen, though, if we confused the abstraction with the thing. Could you actually drink a liter or pour a gallon?

To take another example, consider that language is merely a set of conventions. A given word is solely and only a symbol of something else. Like other abstractions it is only a mental construct. Things to which it refers are real, but it itself is not. Hence, the word "tree" is surely not a tree. If spoken, "tree" is only a sound; if written, only a smear of ink. Apples do not grow on the word "apple tree" and several instances of the word "tree" cannot be cultivated to produce the paper on which this book is printed.

This point must be carried one step further to a rather less obvious conclusion. As we have seen, the lack of correspondence between symbol and referent implies that the former are ultimately unreal. Symbols, whether words, mathematical operators, or concepts more generally, require duality, as we have also seen. But if duality is merely an aspect of concepts, and if concepts are unreal, then clearly duality is also unreal. Thus, the world does not consist of hot and cold, north and south, left and right. Nor does it contain mothers and children, books and readers, planets and satellites. These are all conceptual—dualistic— categories that simply do not obtain in reality. In the same way, there are neither abstractions nor actual things, in that these notions are themselves mere abstractions.

The world, then, is not divided into a set of discrete objects. The tree cannot be separated from the ground in which it grows, the air that surrounds its branches, or the sunlight that nourishes it. However, the fact that the world is not discrete does not imply that it is continuous, in that both adjectives are more dualistic categories. The world is not a unified, holistic unity, for unity is again another conceptual abstraction differentiated from multiplicity. Reality is neither discrete nor continuous, neither a unity nor a multiplicity. Reality, in fact, is not reality, in that to call it real is to differentiate it from the unreal or the illusionary, which is of course another dualistic interpretation.

What, then, is the world? To quote Lao-tzu, "I do not know its name, but call it by the word 'Tao.'" In terms of conventional language this tells us nothing, because "all is the Tao." We have no differentiation, no true concept, and thus no information about what the Tao is. That, of course, is the point—you don't know what the universe is except that it is not divided into categories or separate objects. The most descriptive explanation, though, comes directly from Buddhism. Borrowing from Sanskrit, we obtain the word *tat*, a cognate meaning "that," and continue by describing the world as *tathata*, or simply "thatness." It is the equivalent of refraining from indulging in language altogether, a semantic representation of shaking your head and pointing at the world. The universe is simply that, neither more nor less.

On top of that world we have placed the ordering principles of our various concepts. Yet these concepts are entirely mental projections that categorize, divide, and relate. Just as longitude and latitude are projections that artificially divide the Earth in Cartesian (x, y) coordinates, our concepts artificially divide existence. Hence it is sometimes suggested that "all is mind," in that all our conventional ideas about reality—separate objects, causality, logic, and so on—are products of the mind.[6]

The "true" world, the world that exists in the absence of our mental constructs, is something else entirely. It is non-dual—it does not consist of a multitude of separate objects related to one another by the laws of logic. The relationship between these mental artifacts and the "real" world is the same as that of symbols to things. When we mistake the world-as-concepts for the "natural" (i.e., real) world, we are trapped in a phantasm that is no more the universe than a map or globe is the Earth.

29

We can make the same point in a different way. What is "real" is experience in the form of sensory data. Abstractions, the "not-real," are ideas about experience.[7] What we normally think of as things—trees, say—are entirely and only sense perceptions. Nothing can be known to exist or can exist (that is, be real) except perceptions, because our senses inform us only of perceptions, not of things to which these perceptions might (speculatively) refer. The former are experiential and thus real, while the latter are abstractions and hence unreal.

As an illustration, consider students in an elementary physics class observing that a pencil appears to bend when immersed in water. They are likely to conclude that they are being deluded, that what they experience is effectively hallucinatory. They interpret sensory data in terms of concepts—that is, in terms of ideas. Students "know" that pencils are straight and that there is no causal relationship between immersion in water and instantaneous bending, so that the sensory data are clearly wrong. Of course, sensory data are correct by definition—what you experience is what you experience. Disbelief occurs because the data do not conform to the conceptual order we have imposed on the world. In other words, if we insist in seeing a "pencil" in "water" then, yes, our perception is "wrong" but if we see only *tathata*, if we turn our concepts off for a moment, there is neither pencil, nor water, nor bending. There is only whatever there is.

Similarly, light from the sun is reflected back to the earth by the moon, strikes our eyes and is interpreted by the brain. The experience is the awareness of the moon. The abstraction is the idea of the moon, the notion that there is something distinct from my experience—that there is a difference between the light striking my eyes and the moon itself. In terms of reality, there is only awareness. In effect, my awareness of the moon is the moon.

30

In the same way, I experience the present but create the idea of it. In so doing, I stumble upon the past and the future. I cannot experience the future or the past for the simple reason that I cannot experience what does not exist. Time is an abstraction, something built by the mind as a generalization of experience in the same manner that the idea of the moon becomes a generalization of seeing it. But just as surely as there is no "it" apart from the seeing, there is neither future nor past (nor even present). We think there are only because we confuse our ideas with reality.

Each of the above examples seems terribly counter-intuitive. Pencils really do not bend in water, the moon is distinct from our seeing it, and the future surely comes. Yet, these statements are only conceptually true, that is to say, they are not true at all. They do not describe reality but only the relationships among our collective concepts or ideas about reality. To take a mathematical analogy, suppose we have some concept x, such that x is equal to any element in the set of positive numbers. Then, by convention, we define an operation called the "square root," or the number which multiplied by itself equals x. These concepts tell us that if $x=9$ then the square root of x is 3. Does this mean that three is "real"?

It is by this sort of reasoning that we conclude that tomorrow comes or that the moon exists independently of our seeing it. This deduction does not come from our experience, but from our concepts. Time and the moon exist only as artifices within our minds. We believe that they exist in concrete reality only because we have confused the real with the abstract. In the above example, it is apparent that three reflects only the relationship between the concepts of "nine" and "square root": it does not exist in the way that colors, electrons, or the Black Sea do. If we realize that concepts are merely convenient fictions, it is apparent that nine, three, the square root, time, pencils, water, and the moon are all equally fictitious. They do not exist for the same reasons liters and lines of latitude do not.

IV

The proposition that there is a distinction between concepts and reality is itself a concept. But if concepts are not a part of reality, then the notion that concepts are not real is itself not real. In other words, the proposition is a description of reality, but is not itself real. Like many other abstractions, though, it is quite useful, in that it leads to the following valid conclusion:

> Reality can be discovered only by the abandonment of conceptual thinking.

Hence, the essence of Zen is that if we wish to see the non-dual universe in its true form, then we must cease interpreting it dualistically. Instead of relying upon conceptual glasses that distort and confuse, we must experience reality directly. As Marcel Proust once observed, discovering what is real consists in "having new eyes." The same sentiment informs William Blake's familiar admonition that[8]

> If the doors of perceptions were cleansed everything
>   would appear to man as it is, infinite.
> For man has closed himself up, till he sees all things
>   thro' narrow chinks of his cavern.

The point is that our eyes—the doors of our perception—are clouded by conventional, that is dualistic, thinking. To see beyond to what is real, we must emerge from the caverns of convention and reason.

For this reason it is often suggested that Zen is an experience, in that it consists of seeing the world with new, non-dualistic eyes. To put it another way, Zen is the direct experience of reality. We thus define Zen as

a state of consciousness characterized by the
absence of dualistic thinking.

Of course, as should be readily apparent by this point, Zen is not an "experience" or a "state of consciousness" in that these are only more abstractions. We cannot say anything positive about Zen, in that such statements will involve dualistic concepts and hence be strictly wrong. Still, there is nothing wrong with making such statements as long as we keep in mind that, as abstractions, they are only *about* Zen as opposed to *being* Zen.

To fully appreciate the argument thus far, we must carry it to the next logical step: the abstraction of the self.

NOTES

1. The implications of relativity are far too expansive to be adequately discussed here. Two readable and rewarding accounts are Fritjof Capra, *The Tao of Physics* (New York: Bantam Books, 1975) and Stephen Hawking, *A Brief History of Time* (New York: Bantam Books, 1988).
2. For an accessible account of the question of micro-level causality, see David Bohm, *Causality and Chance in Modern Physics*, 3rd Edition (Philadelphia: University of Pennsylvania Press, 1984).
3. Of course, non-contradiction (like all of logic) is a human creation. This is readily seen in the fact that children have to be taught fundamental principles of logic in the same way they are taught language and other social conventions. See Jean Piaget, *The Construction of Reality in the Child* (New York: Basic Books, 1954).
4. To say that a proposition is non-falsifiable is to assert that there is no empirical evidence that would be adequate to render it false. Hence, the suggestion that everything doubles in size every evening is non-falsifiable in that we can imagine no evidence that would show that such did not occur. Following Occam's Razor, we discard propositions of this sort as errors in rational discourse.
5. The definitive non-technical treatment of Godel's Theorem is Douglas Hofstadter's marvelous *Godel, Escher, Bach: An Eternal Golden Braid* (New York: Vintage, 1980). Hofstadter also discusses the relationship between Godel and the liar's paradox.

6. This view is commonsensical in much of Eastern thought. In terms of traditional Western academic philosophy, the suggestion that material objects do not exist apart from awareness of them is associated with the doctrines of idealism (e.g., Berkeley) and phenomenalism (e.g., Hume).
7. Again, while seemingly decidedly Eastern, this notion has a long currency in Western metaphysics. The best classical arguments are from William of Occam and Thomas Hobbes. For a general discussion, see Nelson Goodman, *The Structure of Experience* (Cambridge, Massachusetts: Harvard University Press, 1951).
8. From "A Memorable Fancy, II."

CHAPTER THREE
Escape from Paradox

Though cured of an illusion, I found this disintegration of the personality by no means a pleasant and amusing adventure.

—Hermann Hesse

The value of mystical and transformative states is not in producing some new experience but in getting rid of the experiencer.

—John White

The previous chapter sought to establish a distinction between ideas and existing material objects. Without disputing
the validity of this distinction, one might nonetheless object
that the thesis remains immaterial to consciousness or
day-to-day life. Does it actually matter that there *really* are
no such things as, say, stars? Our sun still seems to rise
and set with comforting regularity. The constellations appear just as before. The interior of the sun still seems to
generate heat at 20 million degrees centigrade. It still appears as though there are some ten thousand billion billion
(10^{22}) stars in the known universe. What possible difference
could it make to realize that these entities are mental
constructs designed to reduce the complexity of experience
to manageable proportions?

Put another way, one willing to accept the notion that
there is a distinction between concepts and reality may
nonetheless feel as if Einstein had convincingly demonstrated that gravity is an invisible fourth dimension. In
terms of our immediate life, such a proposition, however
important in its own way, seems too removed and abstract
from our real concerns. When all is said and done, how does
this affect us? Teeth still decay, time still goes by, bills must
still be paid, and people still continue to die. In sum, one
might accept the argument being advanced in principle, but
still maintain that it is devoid of practical significance. How
does it affect me to know gravity warps space or that the sun
does not exist? How have I profited from this knowledge?

To fully appreciate the distinction between the abstract and the real, we must carry the argument to its logical and entirely non-obvious conclusions. To do so it is necessary to "understand" the distinction in more than a narrow, intellectual sense. The difference between the real and the abstract must be experienced directly and personally.

The road to Zen begins with this experience.

II

While Zen cannot be construed as endorsing or implying any specific psychological theory, it may be helpful to begin our inquiry in the familiar terms of Freudian psychology. Freud's principal insight was to realize that underlying our self-awareness is a set of drives and impulses that are not accessible to the conscious mind. Beneath the apparent self is an arational striving—the "id," or what Schopenhauer called the "will." At the most primitive level, this force concerns sexual gratification and the quest for physical security. More generally, the id follows the instinctual imperative to seek pleasure and satisfaction while avoiding pain and anxiety.

Because the will is blind, animalistic desire, it is not especially effective in obtaining its ends. Because the will is incapable of considering any notion of the future, unable to weigh costs and benefits—in sum, incapable of rationally or efficiently pursuing its goals—our minds manufacture an entity whose purpose is to satisfy the needs of the id. This creation is called the "ego." It is capable of rationality, it considers the appropriate means to a given goal, and it reconciles the demands of immediate gratification with concern for the future.

Modern psychology, Freudian or otherwise, correctly views the ego (coupled with the superego or conscience in strictly Freudian terms) as the seat of identity. The ego is the internal awareness of oneself. It is the center of consciousness that exists from moment to moment, that has memories, and which occupies various roles such as "son," "brother," "American," "writer," and "husband." The ego embodies what we think of as "personality" and "conscience." It is the person who has tastes and values and opinions. It is the person to whom things happen, the person who has thoughts and feelings, the person who thinks, sees, hears, feels, tastes, and smells. In very simple terms, the ego is the self.

It is also the ego that imposes a dualistic framework on a decidedly non-dualistic world. It does so because simplifying the world from the concrete to the conceptual is a wonderfully effective way of satisfying the incessant demands of the id. The ego seeks to categorize and simplify experience by reducing everything to a set of abstractions, because this strategy allows it to understand and control the world, so as to better satisfy the id. If the world can be understood, it can be manipulated. If it can be manipulated, it can be controlled so as to gratify desires. Thus the invention of a world of discrete objects, related by the principle of logic, is a means to the end of satisfying the desire to survive and flourish.

This consensus view of reality is predicated entirely upon ideas, i.e. upon mental constructs that lack any reality independent of the person who makes them. This notion can be seen readily in the example of color. Surely objects do not and cannot have colors, in that what we perceive as color is the reflection of certain frequencies of light that our eyes are sensitive enough to see. With different eyes, we would see different colors. Color is thus not objectively real, but exists only as a function of first, our perception, and second, the interpretation of that perception. More generally, all sensory data is conditioned by the perceiver. Beyond the physical translation of stimuli (by, say, the eyes), we condition experience by conceptual categories. In other words, sensations are converted into usable form, that is knowledge, not only

41

by the mechanics of our sensory organs, but by our mental schemata. To use the argot of the computer, we are limited not only by our physical hardware, but by our mental software as well.

As normally understood, the world is thus only an idea or set of ideas. It is devised—artificed—by the ego as an instrument with which to pursue the goals of the id. To see or experience the reality of that creation, it is necessary to realize that the ego is itself a contrivance of the id or will. Put another way, to genuinely understand the distinction between the real and the abstract, between reality and the spectral inventions of the ego, it is necessary to see that the ego is itself a fiction.

III

The id is simple in a literal sense of that term. It makes no distinction between sensory inputs and the source of those inputs. Similarly, it does not distinguish between subject and object, i.e., it does not differentiate the self-which-desires from that which is desired. As Freud might put it, the id does not know the external world as such. Instead, it knows only itself, or rather, its own wants, which is the equivalent of all that exists. The ego arises because it becomes useful for the maintenance of the organism to posit an external world. Having done so, the ego acts as the interface between the id and this exogenous fantasy world. It serves to manage and regulate commerce with the external.

Seen in this light, it is apparent that the ego, like the abstract world it manufactures, is synthetic. The reason that the ego creates the external world is the same that leads to the advent of the ego itself. Or, to put it differently, the same imperatives that lead to imposing an artificial, conceptual structure on experience also dictate that we create an illusory self. In effect, this means that we reduce ourselves to an abstraction for the same reason that we reduce the external world to abstractions: because it is useful to do so.

In retrospect, this process is entirely obvious. For our other abstractions to be of value, it is necessary to have an abstracted notion of ourselves. Agriculture, for example, has certain obvious advantages for survival, but to think in terms of a future in which you will have need for food necessitates that you have an idea of the self. In general, any attempt to satisfy the needs of the id requires a concept of the self—in essence, an awareness that there is a person who has needs.

From the perspective of Zen (and here we part company with Freud to join that of Sartre), the basis or ground of the mind is deeper—or at least, broader—than the id. The "true" mind is (human) consciousness, that is (human) awareness. It is the ability to perceive and interpret sensory data. One of the things of which it may be aware are various stimuli resulting from the organic nature of the body. We are then aware of the needs of the id as they occur, in the sense that we experience these. Put another way, the basis of the mind is the ability to experience. The id is just another source of experience, so that we experience the id in the same way we experience a toothache or our own thoughts. Ultimately, the mind is nothing more, or less, than this capacity for experience.

It follows, then, that the person who has experiences does not exist. Instead, there are only the experiences as they occur. The miracle of the ego is the mind's realization that it exists from moment to moment, so that it is helpful to consider that fact in the drive to satisfy desire. The ego is thus abstracted from the true self, i.e., from the stream of experiences that constitute the self. In this sense, the ego is the mind's idea of itself.[1]

Because the content of experience is continuously changing, we tend to identify with the ego, in that it seems a constant. The ego always exists, it has a continuity of experience, so that it seems a fixed point of reference in an otherwise incoherent series of sensory events. As the ego accumulates memories and comes to occupy certain socially defined roles, we tend to see these memories and roles as constitutive of our identity.

IV

It seems entirely odd to suggest that ego is just another fictional idea. Yet, viewed disinterestedly, it seems impossible to quarrel with that judgement. The ego is nothing more than a set of ideas lodged within the consciousness. It has no greater reality than other ideas, in that, by definition, ideas are non-material, mental constructs that exist only within the subjective awareness of the individual. The only difference between "true" ideas and "false" ones—say, between the notion that the earth orbits the sun and its reverse—is that we believe one to be true and one false. So, the real distinctions between ideas are our own ideas about such ideas. In terms of concrete, physical reality all ideas are unreal, in the sense that they have no independent reality apart from our imagining them.

One can imagine demons, devils, and satyrs, but the fact that we have ideas of such things does not imply that they exist as anything except empty fantasies. Similarly, we can imagine vampires, but that does not mean such creatures exist. Of course, if we believe they exist, our thoughts and actions can be affected in peculiar ways, just as the behavior of psychotics is affected by their confused perceptions of reality.

The same reasoning applies to the ego. We have this idea of the self, but this in no way implies that this self exists. The belief in the idea of the self is analogous to the belief in vampires. In both instances, an individual so believing mistakenly takes mental constructs for existing things, with potentially dire consequences. In sum, the fact that we believe in the referents of the ideas in no way demonstrates that such referents exist. However, the very delusion that they are real can cause us to act as if they were real.

To take another example, consider the mind or personality of another person. Can you point to it or touch it? The traditional position is that this personality is intangible, but nonetheless existent. This, of course, begs the question, in that to say something is intangible is to say that it has no material existence—that it exists in some non-materially, i.e., ideal, way. Alternatively, it could be suggested that the personality, like all thoughts, exists as bio-electrical phenomena, i.e., a firing of neurons, that occur when one thinks something. However, this is to suggest only that thoughts have a material basis in the person who has them, not that the referents of the thoughts are themselves real. Clearly, the fact that I have a thought, which is isomorphic to certain brain phenomena, says only that the phenomena are real, not the thing thought about.

Surely this is obvious. Thoughts and real things differ in the same way that literary characters differ from living, breathing persons. Both are creations of the human mind that have no material existence. Put another way, they (like other mythical creatures) do not exist outside of the imagination of the person who imagines them. Your identity, like that of Don Quixote, is a fictional creation devoid of life. It is convenient and rewarding to think about such persons, but it is madness to believe that they actually exist.

Still, the notion that "you" do not exist is understandably difficult to accept. Nothing seems more self-evident and obvious than one's own existence. Descartes's dictum "I think, therefore I am" seems beyond doubt. At a minimum, it certainly *seems* to be true.

Of course, the fact that something seems incontrovertibly true says nothing about its actual truth value. The world certainly seems to be flat, yet we know it to be spherical. The earth appears to be stationary, yet it is moving through space (relative to the sun) at 90 miles per second, while simultaneously rotating on its axis at 900 miles per hour. The book you are reading, the chair you may be sitting on, and you yourself are all seemingly solid objects; in fact, these things are composed almost entirely of the empty space between molecules, atoms, and sub-atomic particles.

As the above examples attest, reality does not always conform to our intuitions. The dictates of common sense all too often fall victim to the frailty of our perceptions. In the following section we attempt to demonstrate directly that the ego is another of these perceptual illusions.

V

If all distinctions, all division into concepts of "this" and "not-this" are arbitrary, then it is clear that the dualistic distinction between "me" and "not-me" is false. To define myself as an ego in relation to the universe is simply another abstraction, another arbitrary division of complex reality into simpler abstractions. Just as there is no real distinction between a tree and the earth in which it stands, there is no distinction between myself and the earth under my feet. Thus, like all dualistic distinctions, the one between yourself and the remainder of the world is intelligible and meaningful only within your mind. It is not a function of reality itself.

If the ego is seen to be an arbitrary invention, it becomes clear that you are simply and only your experience. Life is literally a mirror, where everything that you experience is as much you as anything else. Seen in this way, you are the things of which you are aware. Rather than a person to whom things happen, you are the things themselves. More literally, you are not only the sound of music, the light of the stars, the feel of the earth beneath your feet, you are (in the absence of dualistic distinctions) precisely the music, the stars, the earth.

46

The ego is the abstraction from these experiences. It is the idea of hearing music, seeing the stars, feeling the earth. In contrast, you are these things. Put another way, you are awareness, while your ego is an abstraction formed from the continuity of awareness. The view of the self as an enduring center of experience, linked from one set of experiences to another, is an idea, an abstraction. The real "you" is just the things that "your" mind is aware of. Accordingly, there is no distinction between knower and known, in that you are precisely what you know or feel.

Experiences, then, do not happen to you, for you are precisely and only experiences. Hence, being frightened is not something that happens to me, it is me; I am the feeling of being frightened. By the same token, I am the awareness that the monitor of the computer at which I am typing is a very striking shade of blue. I am the fatigue in my fingers from excessive typing. I am the sound of the keys striking. My image of myself as the person who writes, who has pain, and who hears things is only an abstraction, as is this voice inside my head that makes decisions and which I think of as myself.

In terms of everyday consciousness, we regard this person as a control mechanism. As we have seen, this is in fact the function of the ego, i.e., it regulates our actions so that we do things that are "right" or "good." Hence, this ego constantly seeks things out—to control us, to control our environment, to prepare for the future, and, in order to do all these things, to understand the world. All of this is seeking, i.e., seeking to control, manipulate, and, ultimately, understand.

The easiest way to see the ego for what it is is to realize that it is not necessary to seek. If you let go, if you just stop seeking and let things be of themselves, you will cease conceptualizing. By so doing, you will face reality directly without the benefit of your simplifying assumptions.

The question, though, is how to do this. Given that your seeking is everything you normally think of as yourself, it becomes extraordinarily difficult to imagine being able to stop seeking, in that to do so is to be rid of yourself. In the absence of sedation, sleep, or death, there is no immediately obvious way of turning yourself off.

As an experiment, suppose you try. By doing so you are implicitly "feeding" the ego by seeking after its object of desire. Any attempt to let go of your mind must necessarily fail, because you are consciously trying to control your mind so as to stop controlling it. You are trying to act spontaneously, with the control mechanism of the ego still switched on. But how can you do this, how can you decide to be spontaneous, in that the decision itself implies that you are not being spontaneous? The paradox is that the very act of not controlling your mind is in fact an act of will, an act of volition, an act of control.

The escape from paradox lies in the realization that if you cannot let go of your mind, if you must be in control of it, then you are already acting spontaneously. In other words, if an activity is beyond your conscious control, then you are by definition being spontaneous. If you cannot, by an act of will, decide whether or not to control your mind, then your mind cannot possibly be controlled by you. In considering this process, your ego illustrates its own superfluousness.

The notion of spontaneous control is hardly revolutionary. We recognize a great deal of physiological functions as beyond our conscious control. We do not decide to have our heart beat, to breathe, or to hear sounds. We digest food and convert that food to biochemical energy without deciding to. We perform these and countless other activities automatically, without supervision by the ego.

It also appears that this spontaneity extends to putatively voluntary decisions. Ultimately, you merely make decisions—you don't first decide to decide. As Alan Watts has observed, if this were not the case, there would be an infinite

48

regress of decisions to decide. Given that this does not occur, all decisions somehow just "happen" spontaneously.[2] This is seen most keenly when one has to react without reflection, as in sport or other improvisational activities, like dance or jazz. A dervish, for example, no more decides each movement than a batter decides exactly when and where to swing the bat. Instead, they dance and swing bats. Whether we realize it or not, all activities, from swimming to thinking, happen without the aid of the ego.

Indeed, one of the attractions of many recreational activities is that they allow no role for the ego. To one degree or another, people play music, dance, or engage in sport for the sake of losing the self—for escaping, however temporarily, from self-awareness. A good dancer is not aware of the self in the act of dance, nor is a good pitcher thinking about the self when hurling a baseball. Concentration is focused on an activity, on the experience itself, rather than on the person performing the activity and having the experience. This is the same function that chanting is meant to serve in many Eastern spiritual disciplines: the activity precipitates a state of consciousness in which individuals quite literally lose themselves.[3]

In retrospect, the irrelevance of the ego is so obviously true that it seems almost trivial, as witnessed by the fact that conscious decisions do not make things happen. My desire to finish this sentence will not cause the words to come or my fingers to type. One does not catch a baseball or tie one's shoes by deciding to do so, by willing it to happen. Instead, one catches a ball or ties a pair of shoes by moving one's hands in the appropriate fashion. These activities, like speaking and writing, are managed by the "natural" or non-conceptual mind rather than the ego and, like all other events, occur spontaneously.

To say that things happen spontaneously is not to suggest they occur at random or without reason, but only that they occur spontaneously *relative to the ego*. To draw an analogy,

49

the setting and rising of the sun occur for reasons, but they are surely unaffected by your desires. Because you play no role in determining the orbit of the earth about the sun, the sun rises and sets spontaneously relative to you. Similarly, all "your" efforts to control "yourself" are in vain, in that your decisions, like your digestion of food, are beyond conscious manipulation. Your decisions are your own, but are nonetheless spontaneous relative to your ego.[4]

This can be easily seen if you do in fact take pains to stop controlling your mind. You will discover that you suddenly find yourself "back" in control after a few moments, so that you have to concentrate on not being in control. As you do so, it will become painfully apparent that there is only the mind. This person who stands somehow apart from the mind, this person who is temporarily untethering it for the sake of argument, is exposed as a conceptual error.

The process can be explained in a slightly different way. You normally think of yourself as in control, i.e., you keep your thoughts and desires and actions under control. There is someone—you in the form of your ego—who exercises this control, who grasps the mind for its own purposes. So, then, you are told to stop grasping, to stop seeking or desiring. You then try to stop. But, in attempting to not grasp or attempting to not desire, you are, in fact, grasping at not grasping and desiring not to desire. It seems, then, impossible to stop.

As before, this realization is the key to understanding. Consider that if you were in fact desiring to desire, you could presumably stop. If you were grasping something, you could presumably let it go. But we have just seen that this appears logically impossible in terms of the mind. The obvious conclusion is that you were not grasping, not in control, to begin with—or, equivalently, there is nothing to be let go of.

The ego-illusion results from the mind trying to capture itself, much like a dog chasing its own tail. Just as there is no tail apart from the dog, there is no ego apart from the mind. Hence, the ego cannot control the mind for the same reason that the dog cannot catch its own tail. The same problem occurs in the so-called liar's paradox encountered in the preceding chapter. When the liar says that he is lying in telling you so, he has committed the error (however self-consciously) of using a sentence to say something about itself. We commit the same error when we attempt to control the mind with itself, i.e., with the ego. Just as a sentence cannot assess its own truth value, the mind cannot control itself. Our doomed attempts to exercise such control results from falsely imagining that the ego exists independent of the mind, like the hapless canine who makes the same mistake about his own tail.

In both cases, the trouble is an impossible attempt to always abstract one more level. The liar's statement that he is lying is paradoxical precisely because it is self-referential. The sentence simultaneously expresses and judges the same proposition, so that it is not only a statement, but, at the same time, a statement about a statement. In the same way, the ego is an attempt to abstract from the mind, so that we try simultaneously to think and think about thinking, to both experience an event and experience the experience of it. The self in the form of the ego is the attempt to do precisely this. Given that it obviously cannot be done, the result is confusion and frustration.

The source of all our difficulties, then, is this very odd notion that there is some level of awareness (the ego) abstracted from experience (the natural mind). When the impossibility of this is understood, when we feel in an immediate way that we cannot simultaneously experience and abstract from experience, it becomes apparent that there is no person standing behind and thus in control of the mind. There is no person who "has" a mind and who "has" thoughts. The distinction between the mind and the person who has a mind, between thoughts and the thinker of thoughts, between experience and experiencer, is seen as a misconception. As such, it disappears into the fiery inferno of logical necessity beside four-sided triangles and square circles. This realization is enlightenment, or in Japanese, *satori*.

We cannot comment on the nature of this experience, aside from asserting its transcendence of all conceptualization (and hence all language).[5] Thus, its substance cannot be understood—or rather, it cannot be understood conceptually, in the way one understands Freudian psychology, differential calculus, or the phases of the moon. Instead, it must be experienced directly, so that one comes to understand it in much the same way that one understands how to breathe, walk, or blink.

VI

Doctrinaire differences aside, *satori* embodies the principle of liberation—what in yoga is called *moksha*. It is a state of consciousness in which the self is liberated from the suffering and dissatisfaction inherent in the ego-illusion. In seeing the world directly, it becomes apparent that what we have called the problem of life springs not from the quality or character of life, but from the human effort to understand that life. *Satori*, then, produces *moksha* by freeing the self from the webs of abstraction.

This freedom is found in an escape from the ego's preoccupation with things that are not real. Attention and being are focused away from abstractions, concepts, words, symbols, and ideas and toward the actual concrete world of existence. Zen thus removes the mental clutter that, as William Blake suggests, clouds the doors of perception to the true nature of existence. While we cannot discuss or describe the substance of that existence, we can sketch some of the consequences that flow from the experience of it.

The most immediately obvious of these is the loss of the self. In losing your ego, you also lose its obsessions, its worries, its fears. It is the ego which takes social conventions seriously, and so the ego that believes that social norms have meaning. It is the ego which is concerned with social status, with making a good impression, with being liked and admired. It is your ego which takes offense at the unconventional behavior of others, which is afraid to laugh or cry or scream, which becomes jealous or envious. It is the ego that has pride, that is willing to wage war, that is willing to elevate its own values to the status of Truth.

As abstractions, all ideals are will-o'-the-wisps or ghosts, the pursuit of which is both pointless and potentially destructive. The search for happiness and virtue, security and wisdom, are lamentable by-products of the ego's emphasis on symbols rather than realities. When all is said and done, who is there to be happy or virtuous? Who will take advantage of this wisdom? Who, precisely, will be secure?

The death of the ego is also liberating in the sense that it frees one from the guilt and pain that the self carries within it. In many ways, these emotional scars become integral to the self, so that we define ourselves in terms of past transgressions and unpleasant experiences. The pain that we inflicted on others, and they on us, are ever present in our psyches. The past becomes a burden, like the chains that bind the ghost of Dickens's Jacob Marley. In rejecting the ego, it is seen that these chains are imaginary. Just as there is no person in control of us, there is no person who has sinned or been the victim of sin.

More generally, it becomes apparent that the past, the future, and even time itself, are phantoms. Without an ego, I am my awareness rather than one who is aware. I do not comment on the fact that the substance of "my" awareness appears to be changing, in that as it changes, I change. Without an abstract me, there is no one to label the flow of experience as change or to recognize that this moment was not the same as the last. Thus without an ego, I am no longer a constant in a stream of change. Instead, I am that stream. If I am free of dualism, then I am, in a sense, time. The point is simply that without an ego, the abstractions of future and past are wiped away, leaving only the present.

In being free of time, I am also free of death and the fear of the future. Not only is there no future, there is no one to fear death. The end of life is simply the end of awareness, and I surely cannot be aware of not being aware. The ego is rightly frightened by death because it wrongly views awareness, and consciousness more generally, as something it possesses. Given that death means the end of such possession, that is, the end of the person who possesses life, it is to be feared and loathed. A person without an ego has no such fear, in that he or she "has" neither consciousness nor life. The nothingness of death is nothing to be feared, in that one is already nothing. As is sometimes suggested, Zen solves the problem of death by "dying" first, i.e., by killing the ego, so as to get on with the task of living.

VII

The ego exists as a second-order phenomenon of consciousness. It emerges from consciousness, i.e., awareness, because it is an extraordinarily effective instrument in our instinctual efforts to seek pleasure and avoid pain. Accordingly, the ego is a natural aspect of the human mind. It becomes inimical to sanity only because we chronically lose sight of its status as an instrument or tool of the true self. In coming to see the ego for what it is, we are freed from the confusions it promulgates.

To accept the non-reality of the ego is not to reject it, but only to recognize its limits. By the same token, Zen does not suggest that in denying the reality of time, we do not plan for the future, or that in not fearing death, we act contrary to the dictates of self-preservation. Instead, we recognize these abstractions as just that: abstractions, which, however useful, are not ultimately real. The ego is thus not to be spurned, but viewed as a convenient analytic device. In so doing, we make the ego our tool, rather than the reverse.

NOTES

1. Freud held the ego to be real, to the extent that it was a functional, constitutive component of the mind. In his view, the ego emerged from the id, but operated independently in the sense that the ego was the home of reason and temperance. The view implicit in Zen (and Buddhism in general) is that the ego is just another idea generated by a natural, integrated mind. Hence, as we shall see, the ego is an ineffectual illusion that plays no direct role in decision making (though, like other conceptual errors, it can have indirect effects). In this way, the various functions of the ego are subsumed by the natural mind. What we will call the ego-illusion results from the failure to appreciate this fact.
2. Alan Watts, *The Way of Zen* (New York: Vintage, 1989).
3. The trancelike state of "speaking in tongues" in charismatic Christian sects serves a similar function, as does the more dignified practice of contemplative meditation in the Catholic tradition.
4. This is not to imply that one does not make reasoned decisions or that one does not deliberate. Rather, the point is that ultimately you must decide and that you do this without a conscious decision to do so, in much the same way you make no conscious decision to breathe.
5. By this point, it should be apparent why *satori* is not strictly an "experience." To suggest that it is, implies that there is someone who has such an experience. In the same way, the reader will recognize that the provisional definition of Zen as a state of consciousness is incorrect, for such a definition again implies there is someone who has consciousness. It also asserts that Zen is consciousness, as opposed to not-consciousness.

CHAPTER FOUR
Meaning and Existence

Men do not think that they know a thing till they have grasped the "why" of it.

—Aristotle

All interpretation, all psychology, all attempts to make things comprehensible, require the medium of theories, mythologies, and lies; and a self-respecting author should not omit . . . to dissipate these lies so far as may be in his power.

—Hermann Hesse

Science is the process by which human beings attempt to understand reality. Science is thus a method for developing knowledge that people find useful in interacting with and controlling their environments. Put another way, science is the development of ideas about reality. In this sense, we are all scientists, in that we are continuously creating and testing propositions about the world and ourselves.

The basic building blocks of science are conceptual frameworks—cognitive maps—by which we organize experience. Because the totality of experience is clearly too complex to be understood directly, we "morselize" it into more easily processed pieces. By definition, to conceptualize is to do exactly that: to divide experience into small, abstract bits that are differentiated from other such bits. As the set of our conceptions becomes more complex, we subject all experience to this process, so that sensory data become interpreted entirely in these terms. When data are encountered that do not fit neatly into existing conceptual schemes, we create new ones to accommodate them. By this process, the world is divided into discrete processes and objects related by the principles of reason.

From this foundation, we construct theories. In conversational English, a "theory" implies a hypothesis that one suspects to be true. Hence, one might have a theory that, say, the Japanese dominate the consumer electronic market because they have a planned economy, or because their workers are more productive than their American or West European counterparts. In its scientific usage, though, a theory is a set of propositions through which one is able to predict and manipulate the future. Theories tell us what to do if we wish to achieve certain results by making explicit presumed causal relationships among specific concepts.

We make use of such theories in hundreds of activities every day. Whether aware of it or not, we all have theories on how to drive automobiles, dress, bake bread, write letters, answer phones, and read books. In each case, our theories generate rules that allow us to manage complex tasks with relative cognitive economy. Like all theories, they thus simplify reality by reducing it to more easily understood mental constructs. That simplification, of course, is the entire point of theories, in that to be of any utility, theories must be less complex than the realities they attempt to explain. If one could process information intuitively or unconsciously, there would be no need for a theory. If, for example, we unconsciously "understood" astrophysics, we would not need theories about planets, stars, and moons. If we could grasp intuitively that planets follow elliptical orbits, we would have no need for the concept of planets or orbits, much less a theory of gravitation to deduce the shape of such orbits. It is precisely because we cannot understand the world holistically that we have to invent dualistic concepts that our minds are capable of processing.

To take another example, as individuals (as opposed to physicians), we do not need a theory on the mechanics of food digestion, in that we have no need to understand the process conceptually. Because we need not consciously direct enzymes or the operations of the intestinal tract, there is no necessity for breaking the process into bits small enough for our minds to understand. By the same token, we do not direct our blood to flow, our hearts to beat, or our eyes to see. In writing these words, I need not consciously know how I make my fingers touch the keys, nor must I will the neurons in my brain to fire in the proper fashion so as to form thoughts and sentences. Because I can do these

60

things instinctively, reactively, and unconsciously, I do not "know" how to do them, in that to "know" is to imply a conceptual and theoretical understanding that is both superfluous and impossible.

In any case, to say that one "understands" is to suggest that one comprehends certain mentally constructed abstractions. Given that abstractions are ephemeral creations of the mind, understanding becomes second hand, in the sense that it is in terms of something other than the thing itself. Thus to understand sight, for example, is to appreciate the phenomenon from the distance of abstractions, that is, through something other than sight. More bluntly, to understand the structure of the eye and the method in which the brain interprets visual stimuli is not to see. Theoretical understanding stands in contrast to experience, so that one is continuously attempting to substitute the conceptual for the experiential. This is necessary, from a scientific perspective, because only concepts, rather than experience, can possibly be "understood."

Our minds thus act much like computers, in that to process information it is necessary to convert data into the "digestible" form of binary numbers. Just as a computer can only operate with data that have (in effect) been converted into binary, the usual operations of our conscious minds require dualistically processed information. To reason means to invoke principles of logic, which implies deducing relationships among dualistic mental categories. Put differently, to "understand" experience is to be able to interpret it conceptually. Such interpretation requires first, that we have an appropriate conceptual framework, and second, that we have a theory which draws (conceptual) conclusions from this framework.

The theory of evolution depends upon a variety of pre-theoretical concepts such as "nature," "selection," "organism," and "environment." With the aid of elementary logic, it assembles these notions into a coherent description of the development of biological life. The resulting theory predicts and explains such development through the mechanism of natural selection, whereby species evolve distinctive characteristics as those individuals with the most adaptive characteristics come to dominate the gene pool. From this, we deduce falsifiable hypotheses, which we then test against observation. To the extent that these hypotheses are confirmed, we are confident in the ability of the theory to explain the phenomena in question.

Still, evolution remains only a theory. The debate over whether evolution is a "fact" is misplaced, in that we cannot assess the truth value of theories. Instead, we can only determine whether evolution better conforms to our dualistically processed observations than any competing theory. In other words, we begin with certain basic and uncontroversial concepts, from which we attempt to determine which theory (composed of these concepts) best conforms to experience. Evolution predominates over "creationism," in that the latter theory is rather less successful in accounting for observational data. Ultimately, though, neither evolution nor creation are "true," in that they are merely products of the human mind. Neither are basic properties of reality, in that they, like all concepts and theories built from them, are artifacts of the human attempt to understand experience.

Theories are thus "models" of reality. We create such models precisely because we cannot understand reality itself. Just as the model of the Bastille that you can hold in your hands is not the actual building, neither are theories of reality actually real. To take another example, Crick and Watson determined the structure of DNA by building various models of the molecule, yet these constructions were surely not DNA. In the same way, a theory of gravity is not gravity, a theory of justice is not justice, and a theory of relativity is not relativity.

Because theories are only models, they cannot be judged as right or wrong. As models, they lack essential features of reality, and so in no way can be deemed true or false. Instead, we say that theories are more or less useful, in the sense that they are better or worse in resembling experience or predicting the future. Thus one model of the Bastille is better than another because it more closely resembles the actual structure, not because one is right and the other wrong. Similarly, before Copernicus, it was thought that planets had circular orbits and that the solar system was geocentric. This theory was able to predict the orbits of the planets with great accuracy, but suffered from certain problems. Among these was retrograde motion, or the apparent tendency of planets to sometimes move backwards along their orbital paths. The Copernican system, positing elliptical orbits and the sun as the center of the solar system, supplanted this geocentric theory because it provided better predictions, e.g., by accounting for (and predicting) retrograde motion. From the perspective of scientific inquiry, the fact that Copernicus postulated a heliocentric solar system is largely irrelevant. The critical point is that such an assumption leads to better predictions—that is, it appears to better fit the available data.[1]

Still, it seems odd to suggest that the fact that the Earth *really* does orbit the sun is irrelevant to the utility of the Copernican model. Yet, it is entirely obvious that—as conceptual abstractions—planets, suns, and orbits do not exist in any case. Thus, any statement about the earth is itself already false, in that the earth is a convenient fiction. All science, all reason, all language, depend upon the analysis of concepts that have no real existence. If the sun does not exist, what possible sense can it make to argue over whether it orbits the equally non-existent earth? In other words, we assume an earth and a sun not because these things in any way exist, but because it is useful to do so. Given that the only rationale for these assumptions is utility, there can be no reason for not making other assumptions that, though seemingly false, are also useful. If all theories are fictions, devised solely because they are useful, how do we choose any one fiction over another on any criteria aside from utility?

To repeat, a theory is not a function of reality but a function of our efforts to understand reality. Because a theory is confined solely to our minds, because a theory is only a set of abstract ideas, all theories are ultimately arbitrary *vis a vis* reality. We utilize them not because they are "true," but because they are useful. In the same way, we choose one theory over another not because one is more true than another, but because one is more useful than another.

This view, implicit in the modern philosophy of science, dates back at least to Hobbes. Much like Descartes, Hobbes found himself awash in the radical skepticism that the then dominant view of a mechanistic universe implied. For science to be possible, it was necessary to carve out a portion of the world—a set of ideas, in effect—that was not subject to mechanistic causation. If these ideas were free of determinism, that is, if we were capable of creating and revising them at will, then they could be compared to and tested against the deterministic processes at work. Hobbes clearly understood that these ideas could not be natural to the universe, for if they were, they would be determined and hence useless. Instead, such ideas would have to be created by the mind, for such creations are the only entities about which we can have certain knowledge. In other words, I can be certain only of the "things," i.e., the mental constructs, of which I am the cause. As Descartes incorrectly argued that he could not be deceived about his own existence, Hobbes correctly maintained that he could truly understand only those things which originated in his own mind.

All scientific knowledge, then, is a product of our minds, rather than a product of the universe. Scientific theories are thus "constructed," so that when we "know" something we are, in fact, the origin of that knowledge. The world so constructed has no cause aside from our minds, in that the only things we can possibly know are those that we have created. Accordingly, the entire world as we *know* it is, and must be, an artifact of the mind.

More generally, given that the world does not consist of abstractions, the creation of such abstractions is inherently arbitrary. There are very good reasons for creating conceptual abstractions, but one set of abstractions cannot be justified over any other except by the principle of utility. To take an example from symbolic systems, we might say that Arabic numerals are more useful than Roman, because mathematical operations are easier in the former system. In terms of efficiency, European languages are more easily read and written than those based on ideograms (e.g., Chinese). Similarly, we can say that using a calculator is an easier way of taking cube roots than using a slide rule, that word processors are more versatile than typewriters, and that a computer is faster than an abacus. In no case, though, can we categorically say that any of these things are somehow "better" in an absolute sense. They are better only in regard to certain arbitrary characteristics.

In the same way, no method of conceptualizing can be objectively superior to any other. There is nothing in the structure of the universe that dictates how to abstract from experience, so that all methods of abstraction are arbitrary in relation to reality. We judge schemes of abstractions based on their utility and nothing else.

In economics, for example, we often assume a scenario, called a "market," in which individuals are free to buy and sell without interference. Given certain other assumptions, such as perfect information and the absence of monopoly, it is quite easy to demonstrate that markets lead to an optimal distribution of goods in which supply equals demand. As all economists recognize, there are no such things as markets, given that costs accrue in obtaining information, that there are barriers to firms entering markets, and that oligopolies tend to obtain. Still, the idea of the market is remarkably useful, and economists cling to it regardless of its obvious "falsity." All economic models rely upon similar assumptions (e.g., rational agency) that are known to be false. These models are justified not because citizens tend to conform to the economic definition of rationality, i.e., not because the assumptions of the model are in any way "true," but because such assumptions yield interesting results.

All theories rely upon assumptions that cannot be demonstrated to be true, in that all theories rely upon concepts. This, in turn, implies that all theories assume a dualistic world. As we saw in Chapter Two, the world is not dualistic. For that reason, all theories are necessarily "false," in that they depend upon the assumption of dualism—like perfect information or economic rationality—which we know to be false.

Given that all theories share the fundamental assumption of dualism, we can imagine a general theory of reality that forms the foundation for all other theories. This general theory postulates a world of discrete objects that flow through time and are ordered by logic, causality, and so on. For lack of a better term, we call this world "consensus reality." It thus follows that

Consensus reality is an assumption.

That is, it cannot be demonstrated to be "true" or otherwise "real." The world as we know it is assumed not because we can prove it exists, but because it is extraordinarily useful to assume that it does. By believing in an external world that follows deterministic laws, we create a world composed of a series of events in which we are more or less capable of intervening. By manipulating the causes of events, we alter the course of experience from what it otherwise might be.

To take an obvious example, by abstracting from the lack of chemical energy that obtains when our bodies are not allowed to digest food for long periods of time, we create the idea of "hunger." By further abstracting the notion of "food," and determining that hunger ends when we eat, we have gone a long way toward improving the quality (and duration) of our lives. Similarly, by importing additional notions such as seasons, agriculture, and the domestication of animals, we are able to develop highly sophisticated theories for the raising, harvesting, and distribution of food. In sum, by attributing a cause to hunger, we can avoid and control it.

While dualistic assumptions are useful in obvious ways, they remain arbitrary in relation to reality. They have no existence independent of our imagining them, in much the way that clouds have no pattern to them aside from that which we assign them. In other words, dualism cannot be justified from any perspective save utility. Accordingly, we must conclude that

Consensus reality is arbitrary.

Like markets, consensus reality is an analytical device for solving problems. Just as there are no markets, there is no "objective" world aside from our ideas about it. The world of ordinary consciousness, of the ego and convention, is thus without any final *metaphysical* justification. Were it possible to achieve our desired ends by assuming some other sort of world, that world would be preferred—and thus assumed to exist.

II

On occasion, otherwise powerful theories will produce anomalies. This occurs, of course, when theoretical predictions (like planetary orbits) are inconsistent with observable conditions (like retrograde motion). Less obviously, anomalies manifest themselves in paradoxes that arise out of the structure of theory rather than the nature of reality.

This phenomenon is nicely illustrated in an example from a branch of mathematics called game theory. Imagine a situation in which two individuals conspire to commit a felony. To take a historical case, suppose Haldeman and Ehrlichman conspire to cover up the robbery of the offices of the Democratic National Committee. They are initially charged with a felony carrying a sentence of five years. However, there is adequate evidence to send them to prison for only two years on a lesser misdemeanor charge. The prosecution then offers Ehrlichman a plea bargain: if he is willing to confess and turn state's evidence against his co-conspirator, he will be given a sentence of only one year. The same arrangement is also offered to Haldeman.

There are thus four possible outcomes to this "game," depending upon what the "players" elect to do. If both refuse to cooperate with the police, they will both be convicted of the misdemeanor, meaning that each goes to jail for two years. If Haldeman cooperates but Ehrlichman does not, then Haldeman is given one year, but Ehrlichman goes to jail for five. Similarly, if Ehrlichman cooperates while Haldeman does not, then Ehrlichman gets one year and Haledeman five. If both accept the bargain, that is if they both testify against one another, they are each sentenced to four years. This game is aptly called the "prisoner's dilemma," in that each prisoner faces a difficult choice. Given these circumstances, what does a rational player do?

Haldeman examines the situation and discovers that if he refuses to turn evidence, he receives, depending upon what Ehrlichman does, either two or five years. On the other hand, if he cooperates with the police, he receives either one or four years. Hence, regardless of what he expects Ehrlichman to do, Haldeman receives a shorter sentence by cooperating with the prosecution. Ehrlichman, of course, faces precisely the same situation, so that he too will agree to testify for the prosecution. The result is that both testify against each other, so that each goes to prison for four years.

This result is anomalous because each player is imprisoned for a longer period of time than necessary. If each had refused to cooperate, both would have been sentenced to only two years rather than four. As we have seen, though, refusing to cooperate was in fact irrational. Both individuals did exactly what rationality dictated, and, yet, each is worse off than if they had done otherwise. In other words, rational individuals make themselves worse off than if they had been irrational. The implication is clear: in this situtation, it is irrational to be rational.

The assumption responsible for this troubling result is the implicit definition of rationality as self-interested utility maximization. By assuming that individuals act to maximize self-interest, we are forced to conclude that the best way of doing so is not to maximize self-interest. This is nonsense, but there is no escape from the paradox without dropping the theory upon which it is based. Put differently, the anomaly emerges as a necessary part of the theory, so that to save ourselves from it, we must abandon the theory.

Much the same conclusion obtains when we utilize rationality to understand the electoral process. Rational individuals participate in presidential elections for the purpose of assuring that their preferred candidate wins. However, with a potential electorate of 180 million people, the probability of any one person's vote deciding the election is nil. Accordingly, the outcome will be the same regardless of whether or not one votes. Given that and the fact that voting entails costs in terms of time and energy, it is irrational to pay such costs and hence to vote. Seen from this perspective, one has a substantially greater chance of being killed in an accident while going to the polls than in deciding the result.

It is possible, of course, that rational actors might participate anyway if they believed that it is important to maintain the democratic system. One might reason that if everyone failed to vote then the system would collapse, so that it becomes rational to vote, not to determine the course of the election, but to maintain the institution of democracy itself. Yet, this approach leads to precisely the same paradox as before; rational agents will observe that the survival of the system will not be affected by the decision of one individual. If very few people vote, the system will collapse anyway, regardless of what a single person does. Similarly, if many participate, democracy will continue without one's participation. In either case, then, rational individuals will not vote. As in the prisoner's dilemma, the conclusion follows inexorably from the premise. Yet, it is apparent that people do in fact vote, suggesting that the anomaly is a function not of the reality that the theory describes, but of the theory itself.

Although discomforting, the idea that theories contain such anomolies should come as no surprise. To generalize slightly from Godel, no axiomatic system can be complete, i.e., no such system can account for the full complexity of reality. This inability manifests itself (among other ways), in theoretical "worm-holes," such as the proposition that rational individuals are not rational. Unfortunately, all axiomatic systems are plagued by these sorts of internal contradictions.

III

Consensus reality is one such axiomatic system. It begins with a set of *a priori* assumptions, such as temporal succession, causality, and the principle of non-contradiction. From these assumptions, we construct the world by imposing conceptual regularity upon experiential chaos.

What we have called the "problem of life" emerges as an anomaly within this model of reality. Life appears to be a random collection of events perpetuated upon an isolated center of consciousness. Experiences become abstracted, so that rather than being experience, we become the person to whom these experiences happen. Because this person is trapped within a theory that is predicated upon concepts which refer to or signify other things, we attempt to deduce some meaning from experience. The fundamental questions thus become those of the "meaning" of life and the "meaning" or purpose of the person who lives.

Yet, as in all romantic quests, we suspect that the answer cannot be found. No amount of searching will find the Holy Grail, just as no amount of tinkering with the prisoner's dilemma can avoid its conclusion. The problem of life flows directly from the assumptions implicit in consensus reality. We attempt to assign meaning to experience by making experience point to or represent something else. Because everything in consensus reality has a meaning, because everything signifies or stands for something else, we expect life to signify something else as well. Yet, life logically cannot do this, in that life is not a concept. In other words, only conceptual abstractions have meanings. The reality of your existence—the words on the page you are reading, the texture of the paper on which they are printed, the ambient sounds you may be hearing—these things are the "stuff" that constitute your life. They have no meaning aside from themselves. They do not refer to, they do not signify, anything else.

Life cannot be understood, and thus assigned a meaning, because life is not an abstraction. The process of searching for it is thus much akin to the notion of trying to be rational in the context of the prisoner's dilemma, wherein one is trapped in the contradiction of trying to be rational by being irrational. If I am rational, then I must consciously be irrational, but in being irrational, I am in fact being rational, so that I must cease being irrational, so as to be rational, and so on, endlessly. In precisely the same way, the endeavor to understand life, to find its meaning and purpose, is an endless cycle of inaction where the mind desperately tries to clutch at both itself and experience, like a sound trying to hear itself.

This process is sometimes explicated in terms of the false duality between subject and object that is implicit in the

71

idea of the ego. Events and experiences become objectified by the subject who experiences them, so that the subject-self differentiates sensory data by viewing itself as a fixed center capable of discrimination. The "objective world" is thus the set of things objectified by the subject in such a way that they become distinct from, and independent of, the observer-subject.

Because this subject objectifies everything, it attempts to objectify itself, so that it asks "What am I?" or "What is the purpose of my existence?" Now, the very fact that it can ask this question implies that it discriminates between self-as-experience and self-as-experiencer. There thus becomes two selves: one which is inquired about and one which does the inquiry. The self is simultaneously the one studying and the thing that is studied, like the Escher sketch of a hand drawing itself. The self asks who it is, but in asking the question makes itself an object rather than a subject. Given that the subject is in fact searching for a person—that is, for another subject—it can never find such a person, in that the process of searching transforms the desired subject into an object, and hence something entirely different from that which is sought.

The ego thus alienates itself not only from the "external" world of other people and things, but from the mind itself. It does so by breaking the mind in two, with one half (the subject) forever chasing the other (the object). The conditions which give rise to posing the question of the meaning of life are thus precisely those that make answering the question entirely impossible. The problem of life, then, is a necessary consequence of the assumption of a subject-object divison, which is, in turn, a necessary consequence of consensus reality. As Masao Abe explains[2]

> To be human is to be a problem to oneself. . . . To be human means to be an ego-self; to be an ego-self means to be cut off from both one's self and one's

world; and to be cut off from one's self and one's world is to be in constant anxiety. This is the human predicament.

The quest for meaning is thus a classical infinite regress in which the mind cycles back and forth between its falsely divided halves.[3]

IV

To avoid this process of self-delusion, it is necessary to exit the theory of consensus reality. Given that all theories are instrumental rather than "true," they can be modified or abandoned when they become counter-productive. Because all theories are arbitrary, there is no reason to cling to one when it no longer serves a useful purpose. In the present context, it is apparent that there comes a point when consensus reality ceases to be useful. Mental health requires that we know when and how to forsake that reality in favor of the non-dualistic, non-conceptual realm of experience.

To do so, we need a metatheory, or a theory about theories. Godel's Theorem is a metatheoretical result because it is not a theorem (like that attributed to Pythagoras) that is deduced from any particular axiomatic system, but is instead a theorem about axiomatic systems. In terms of reality theory, we can say, metatheoretically, that consensus reality is distinct from the "true" non-dualistic world. Metatheory can also refer to a theory for selecting among competing theories. Occam's Razor is a rudimentary metatheoretical principle, which recommends (other things being equal) simpler explanations over more complex ones. A slightly more elaborate metatheory exists in physics to guide the choice between quantum mechanics and relativity. To simplify somewhat, this metatheory tells us to use the former for studying the micro level (e.g., the atomic and subatomic), but to rely on the latter for the macro (e.g., time-space).

In the present context, we need something like a metatheory for selecting theories of reality, but with the caveat that one of our choices can be the selection of no theory at all. In other words, we need to construct mental software that tells us when to "turn off" all theorizing. Such a metatheory is easily constructed, in that it need only specify those questions which consensus reality is unhelpful in answering. Hence, we need know only when we do and when we do not wish to concern ourselves with the world of convention— that is, when we wish to experience reality rather than attempt to understand it.

As in all theories, though, we do not suggest that this view is in any way "correct," but only that it is useful. Put differently, the idea of the metatheory is introduced because it allows the conceptual mind to begin an attack upon itself—because it provides a mechanism for a mind trapped within conceptual thought to escape that trap. More importantly, if we view consensus reality as a complex axiomatic system, it is entirely consistent to think of that system as producing the conclusion that the system should be (temporarily) abandoned. Theories can and do have "escape clauses" which serve to terminate themselves.

To borrow a metaphor from John Lilly, the mind may be thought of as a "biocomputer" that runs certain "programs."[4] Like all programs, consensus reality can be exited in only two ways: either we turn the machine "off" and begin again, or we work within the context of the current program. Traditional methods, such as the *koan* and meditation (about which we will have more to say later) are examples of the former—they overload our CPU, causing the system to "crash." In proposing the idea of the metatheory, we suggest following the latter course—to exit the conceptual thinking program precisely by conceptual thinking. In either case, the result, to strain the metaphor, is to reach Zen by returning to the "operating system" that forms the non-conceptual mind, i.e., the initial point where no programs are running.

The metatheory thus assumes consensus reality, and implicitly, the ego-self. By taking such a world as given, we come to the point, as this chapter has sought to illustrate, where it becomes apparent that (a) this world is arbitrary, and (b) that the problem of life is an illusory artifact that arises from confusing that arbitrary creation with reality. This, in turn, implies that (c) rationality itself dictates following the path of Zen. The imperative to experience Zen is thus logically derivable within the framework of scientific investigation.

V

Searching for life's meaning is a natural and very human endeavor, but it arises from an error in self-understanding. As we saw in the previous chapter, we are only awareness, yet we appear to be someone who is aware. As a consequence, we attempt to discover who this person is and why he or she exists. Of course, it is impossible to do this in that awareness cannot be aware of itself. If the true self is primal awareness, then the entire notion of discovering a meaning is absurd, for we are life and nothing more. Equivalently, you cannot find a meaning or a value to your experience because you are exactly and only that experience.

Thus, the search for meaning is the result of an imaginary ego mindlessly attempting the impossible, like an ear trying to hear itself hearing. The fact that there is no meaning to be found is not a reason for despair, in that the problem is not in the absence of meaning but in the logical and experiential errors that give rise to the asking of a pointless and irrelevant question. Seeing the problem for what it is, the mind stops its incessant clutching at itself. The concomitant anxiety and confusion disappears. In this manner, the question of the meaning of life is answered.

Such a view is actually similar in many respects to the skepticism of David Hume or the logical positivists.[5] To them, all metaphysical speculation is merely "nonsense to be dismissed." All theories about ontological reality, they argue, are vacuous and empty. By failing to appreciate that fact, we create logical quandaries by confusing the purely emotive question "What is the meaning of life?" with an intelligible interrogative. Anxiety over the lack of a spiritual core to life results from false expectations that arise from taking gibberish to be meaningful sentences. Thus, as Bertrand Russell argued, the goal of philosophy is to liberate ourselves from such pitfalls by clarifying the meaning of language and the concepts they represent.

In much the same vein, Wittgenstein maintained that philosophical problems result from ambiguities inherent in our conceptualizations.[6] In the present context, the confusion and anxiety that result from identifying with the ego are results of the ambiguity in the concept of the self. Seen in this light, Zen is a philosophy of sorts, in that it serves to illuminate this confusion.

NOTES

1. For the general rationale for judging models on the quality of their predictions rather than the "realism" of their assumptions, see Milton Freidman, *Essays in Positive Economics* (Chicago: University of Chicago Press, 1953).
2. Masao Abe, *Zen and Western Thought* (Honolulu: University of Hawaii Press, 1985) p. 6.
3. The demon in this attempt at self-discovery is the mistaken assumption that there exists some kind of inner self which one can become conscious of. The best known defense of such a position is surely René Descartes's dictum that *cogito ergo sum*—I think, therefore I am. By recognizing the possibility of doubting his sense experience, Descartes concluded that he must exist, in that he could hardly doubt his own doubting. The very fact that he was capable of reflection was thought to prove that there was something beyond or above the stream of experience. This conclusion is patently false, in that it confuses the object of consciousness with the subject of consciousness, so that the "self" of which I become conscious is the object of reflection rather than the subject. For a remarkably lucid discussion of this point, see Jean-Paul Sartre, *The Transcendence of the Ego*, translated by Forrest Williams and Robert Kirkpatrick, (New York: Julian Press, 1968).
4. John Lilly, *Progamming and Metaprogramming in the Human Bio-Computer* (Garden City, NJ: Doubleday, 1967).
5. The best reader on logical positivism and its ancedents is probably Alfred Ayer, ed., *Logical Positivism* (Glencoe, Illinois: The Free Press, 1959).
6. For a readable discussion, see G.E.M. Anscombe, *An Introduction to Wittgenstein's Tractatus* (London: Hutchinson, 1971).

CHAPTER FIVE
The Origins of Zen

To bake an apple pie from scratch, one must first invent the universe.

—Carl Sagan

Satori *is, in fact, a matter of natural occurrence, of something so very simple that one fails to see the wood for the trees, and in attempting to explain it, invariably says the very things that drive others to the greatest confusion.*

—Carl Jung

We have hitherto discussed Zen in the terms of Western philosophy and science. Clearly, though, philosophies do not arise spontaneously out of vacuums. Like all social ideas, they evolve over time within a particular cultural and intellectual context. In this chapter, we trace the development of Zen within the context of its origin.

Two caveats apply. The first is the very enormity of the task. Multiple volumes could be (and have been) written on any of the dozens of ideas that this chapter addresses. In an effort to reduce the project to reasonable proportions, our attention will be limited to the intellectual progress of the ideas that have led to Zen. To use Jung's metaphor, this approach may mean missing many of the trees, but we trust that it will make it more difficult to lose sight of the wood.

The second difficulty concerns the twin problems of interpretation and historical reconstruction. The scholarly literature on Eastern thought is, as in so many other disciplines, so riddled with inconsistencies as to be largely inconclusive. For this reason, it is often impossible to make a conclusive case for even comparatively simple issues such as the year of Buddhism's arrival in China, much less about the precise interpretation of this or that text. Rather than losing ourselves in these debates, we will eschew them altogether by abandoning any pretext of a scholarly or complete treatment.

II

The most immediate progenitor of Zen is a set of principles known as Taoism. According to tradition, the founder of this movement is Lao-tzu. While the details of his life (and even the veracity of his existence) are subject to scholarly debate, it is generally agreed that he was a historical figure who lived in China in the sixth century B.C. It is sometimes argued that his proper name was Li Erh, with Lao-tzu being a title of courtesy literally meaning "old (*lao*) philosopher or sage (*tzu*)." In any case, the advent of Taoism as a more or less unified body of thought dates to his volume *Tao-te Ching* (*The Way and Its Power*), though precursors to the ideas expressed in this book enjoyed currency in China long before this synthesis and systematization.[1]

Taoism is a system of liberation from the suffering and confusion inherent in ordinary consciousness. The limiting factor in such consciousness—the prison that one seeks to be liberated from—is social convention. As the word suggests, conventions are collective agreements about how to behave, think, and function. Convention defines language, customs, and the interpretation of experience. We agree among ourselves to divide a tree from the ground in which it stands, and to call the resulting objects "tree" and "ground." In the same way, we define these entities as distinct objects, as opposed to, say, a continuous process of "treeing." While we can recognize some elements of convention, such as the word "tree," others, such as the idea of trees, become so ingrained in our thinking that it becomes difficult to keep in mind that they are only agreements rather than necessary elements of the cosmos. In other words, we confuse the socially defined universe with the actual universe, so that the social order is equated with the natural order.

This confusion is pervasive, so that we tend to conflate cultural, religious, and scientific traditions with reality.

Social ideas such as individuality, the free market, and relativity; social roles such as sister, student, and intellectual; and social practices such as monogamy, shaking hands, and conversation over coffee: these are all conventions that occur solely because, as a society, we have agreed to accept them.

We socialize our children in these norms, teaching them what is and what is not acceptable. We fashion powerful social penalties for failure to comply. Those flouting the more important of these norms (such as property rights) are jailed. Those who transgress only at the margins (as in, say, public flatulence) are merely treated with disdain by others. We thus indoctrinate individuals into thinking in set patterns, while simultaneously establishing incentives (in terms of rewards and penalties) for following these patterns. As a result, there emerges a set of socially defined and socially maintained norms that regulate not only our communal interactions, but our manner of thinking as well.

The most vital aspect of this social conditioning is the identification of both others and self with social roles. We become lawyers, husbands, the middle class, and Americans. We position others as clients, wives, the working class, and foreigners. These social roles, coupled with the rules regulating the behavior of each, form much of our identities, in that they tell us who we are (and how to behave) relative to the environment and each other.

Convention also defines identity in a more fundamental way, in that we have decided to define ourselves in terms of the ego. At its most basic, the self becomes the sum total of one's memories and impressions. Current experiences are things that happen to us, rather than being us. As a culture, we have elected to think of ourselves as these centers of experience, distinct from experience itself.

Lao-tzu's insight was the realization that convention is only convention. Behind the socially determined world is another, more real world. Because it is beyond convention, we cannot use the convention of language to explain or describe it, but, following Lao-tzu we "call it by the word *Tao*."

The *Tao* is the reality underlying the world of dualism and convention. The word literally means "way" or "path," and suggests an image of the way or course of life. To simplify somewhat, the *Tao* is nature in the most expansive meaning of that term. It is the guiding force behind life and all existence—the "mother of everything beneath the heavens." It is the permanent, unchanging unity that belies the apparent multiplicity of forms. The *Tao* is both the totality of all that exists and the reason for such existence. It is the unfolding of a universe that is ultimately a process, an event, and an activity. The *Tao* is the spontaneity of creation, the source from which the world is born. It is the Absolute, the Prime Mover, the Ground of Being. In Aristotelian terms, the *Tao* is the *logos* of all that exists.

In another, slightly different usage, the *Tao* is referred to as nothingness or non-being (*pen-wu*). It is the source from which all things come, the no-thing from which things are born as individuated substances. In English, this concept is sometimes referred to as void, so that it is said that the *Tao* is void. This is in some ways misleading, in that to say "all is void" is not to suggest that nothing exists, but only that reality is void of objects and things as defined by convention. Matter genuinely exists, but it is no longer restricted to the arbitrary categories of convention. It is thus impossible to comprehend the substance of the *Tao*, in that it appears devoid of the entities that populate the world of ordinary consciousness. In other words, there are no longer the abstractions of tree and ground, man and woman, sun and sky, so that the "true" world of the *Tao* is "empty."

As a system of thought, Taoism is the imperative to recognize and live by the *Tao*. Convention is inimical to this endeavor, in that by definition convention is a human artifact that stands in the way of the naturalness and spontaneity that is the *Tao*. To be "in the *Tao*," it is necessary to act in an unaffected, natural way. This requires that we cease conscious attempts to control the mind, in that such attempts must necessarily be unspontaneous. In this sense, "control" implies both the notion of conscious deliberation, and, more important, the ordinary process of thinking in dualistic terms. To use the terminology developed in earlier chapters, this is "letting go" of the mind. Put another way, because the *Tao* cannot be shaped to fit our conceptual categories, because it transcends all convention, dualistic thinking stands in the way of the *Tao*. In Chinese this doctrine is referred to as *wu-wei*, meaning non-action, or really, non-conscious action. *Wu-wei* thus means an unwillingness to let the conscious mind run rampant. To cultivate *wu-wei* is to let things be (including our own minds), in the sense of letting nature, or the *Tao*, run its own course.[2]

By releasing the mind to act on its own, we free ourselves from the confining webs of convention. In so doing, we open ourselves to the flow of the *Tao*, substituting what might be called intuition for the machinations of conscious thought. This reliance upon intuition suggests an absence of self-consciousness in which the mind acts (or thinks or perceives) without reliance upon, or reference to, conventional notions of the self.

Chuang-tzu, a latter disciple of Lao-tzu, explains this phenomenon with the image of "fasting with the mind." By refusing to "feed" the mind by letting it consume or cling to experience, we allow it to function in its intended mode of non-clinging *wu-wei*. He compares the intuitive, non-grasping mind to a mirror:[3]

> The perfect man employs the mind as a mirror. It grasps nothing; it refuses nothing. It receives but it does not keep.

The mind should thus be a mirror which reflects only what it receives. In the same way that a good mirror reveals only

the images that it receives, rather than its own im-
perfections, the properly conditioned mind functions as if it,
too, did not embellish its own texture upon what enters it.
The best mind is one that is not aware of itself, just as the
best mirror is one that does not reflect itself.

In achieving this state of consciousness, we unlock the
hidden power, the vitality of the *Tao*, within us all. Manifested in a person, this force is called *te*. It emerges from the
mind naturally when the constraints imposed by the ego
and conventional thinking fall away. By letting go of the
mind, we free it from the rigid quantification of conceptual
categories. For instance, in music and dance, this occurs by
letting go of the score and playing, or moving, instinctively.
In the same way, good lecturers, as all students know, are
those who are extemporaneous, not those that read verba-
tim from a prepared text. Good dancers, good musicians,
and good teachers are all "in the *Tao*," performing naturally
and spontaneously.

Te also means "virtue," and in this sense can be interpreted in two ways. The first is similar to Aristotle's usage of
the term to denote the internal quality or disposition that
allows individuals to achieve the human purpose or *telos*.
In this way, *te* represents the natural, proper condition of
humanity. *Te* is what we are meant to be, what we must be
if we wish to reach harmony and contentment.

In the second meaning of virtue, *te* implies a natural
saintliness that is to be contrasted with the artificial, hyp-
ocritical virtues of convention. From the perspective of the
Tao, socially defined prescriptions require people to be
insincere, and, hence, immoral. Because conventional morality is internally inconsistent, it is not to be taken seriously. *Te* thus stands in opposition to what is normally
meant by morality or ethics, in that these are ersatz human
inventions that obstruct true virtue. By implication, to be
truly moral, one must renounce all ideas about morality.
The logic is that notions of right action or right thought

cause people to be unspontaneous or inhibited, and thus contrary to the *Tao*.[4]

The lesson of *te* is that we should return to simplicity. We should not acquire possessions, read philosophy, or pursue moral education in that such endeavors merely distance the self from its natural state. Worldly attachments, like devotion to conventional rules of behavior, foster alienation, unhappiness, and self-absorption. Odd as they may sound, such views are not entirely alien to our own cultural experience, as witnessed by the Romantics (such as Shelley) or the Transcendentalists (such as Whitman or Thoreau). In much the same vein, Thomas Jefferson also stressed the superiority of natural and unaffected virtue over the studied and inculcated, suggesting that when confronting "a plowman and a professor" with a moral dilemma "the former will decide it as well and often better than the latter because he has not been led astray by artificial rules."[5] Hence, our goal should be Rousseau's noble savage—the natural man, unpolluted by science, technology, hubris, and the general decadence of modern life.

In Lao-tzu's words from the *Tao-te Ching*:

Banish wisdom, discard knowledge
And you will benefit a hundred fold.
Banish human heartedness, discard morality
And the people will be dutiful and compassionate.

The obvious implication is that our attachment to abstract, conventionally defined notions of wisdom and morality stand in the way of true morality. To find compassion, abandon all ideas about compassion. To discover true wisdom, discard all notions about wisdom. To be virtuous, free yourself from the desire to be so.

Liberation, then, is to be found in replacing the artificialities of convention with the spontaneity of the *Tao* and the power and virtue of *te*. This transformation is liberating in the sense that it frees the self from imprisonment within a socially defined world of conceptual abstractions that have been mistaken for reality. It is a freedom that comes from experiencing and understanding true reality—the *Tao*—personally and directly. In sum, liberation consists in awareness of, identification with, and living in accordance with, the underlying stream of existence called the *Tao*.

Chuang-tzu emphasized this process as seeing the underlying unity of dualistic opposites. Good and evil, true and false, up and down, are all relative. They arise mutually, with one necessarily producing the other. This is nicely symbolized by the universally recognized circle diagram of the *yin–yang*. The black and white each represent a dualistic pole, joined together in an all encompassing unity. They are not opposed, but mutually dependent; they do not hide the *Tao*, but only express it. Dualism, like other ephemera of convention, is falsely imagined and will be resolved in the *Tao*. Emancipation is to see all opposites as synthesized in the unity of the *Tao*.

III

Buddhism arose in the sixth century B.C. as an innovation within the much older Hindu tradition. The canon of Hindu scriptures is known as the *Veda*. It contains a variety of works assembled over a thousand-year period beginning around 1400 B.C. From the perspective of Buddhism, the most important element of this canon is the collection called the *Upanishads*, which were written over several centuries beginning around 800 B.C.

For our purposes, the central aspect of this tradition is a mythological cosmology in which the multiplicity of the universe is a game played by a supreme consciousness. This consciousness, sometimes referred to as *Brahman* or *purusha*, is the sacred, primal force that both forms and sustains the universe. As such, it is the foundation of life and experience. While this force was originally a holistic unity, it chose to scatter itself, to break itself apart into individuated beings. Thus, in the beginning all was the unity of the one, and this one, for the sake of amusement, elected to decompose itself into the world as we know it. However, in the process of decomposition, *Brahman* does not cease to be *Brahman*, in the way that a tree cut into pieces is no longer a tree. In terms of *Brahman*, the sum of the parts is not greater than the whole.

All sentient beings are the eyes and ears of *Brahman*—indeed, they are *Brahman* in a literal sense. Put another way, the sentience of living beings is the sentience of *Brahman*. Since *Brahman* is divine, all beings share in that divinity. In this way, all living creatures are the foundation of the universe and the intelligence that once created and currently guides it. Accordingly, *Brahman* not only exists in individuals, but it is them. At the most basic level, the central message of the *Upanishads* is the doctrine that *Brahman* is the self (*atman*). Thus the true self, the self-as-*atman* or the self-as-*Brahman*, is distinct from, and greater than, the conventional view of the self-as-ego.

There are widely divergent interpretations (or *darsana*) of this point, but within the Vedanta school, spiritual attainment is to be found in discovering, or, rather, recovering, one's self or *atman*. Shankara expresses such a doctrine directly, arguing that since only *Brahman* is ultimately real (*sat*), the ego-self is necessarily illusion (*maya*). There are thus two levels of truth or spiritual awareness, the first or lower is ordinary consciousness, and the second or higher is the identity with *Brahman*.

Entanglement in *maya* implies entanglement in life and the ego. It results from a failure to practice *wu-wei*, and so produces *karma*. Rather than the moral imperative it is sometimes mistaken to be, *karma* is a kind of experiential glue. When one ignores the principle of *wu-wei*, i.e., when one intervenes in life, one generates *karma*, which causes one to continue to intervene, "gluing" one to the world of *maya. Karma* results in an individual being trapped in *samsara,* the so-called cycle of birth-death-rebirth. The *karma* accumulated in one lifetime continues with a person into another life, so that he or she is doomed to live again. *Nirvana* is the escape from this cycle.

As in Taoism, both the *atman* and *samsara* doctrines are teleological, in that they suggest a purposefulness to nature and existence. Crudely put, this goal or purpose is the individual's realization of identity with the absolute and thus his or her liberation from *samsara.* Enlightenment is thus an understanding of one's actual nature, implying an awareness that one shares in the divine. This experience is called *moksha,* meaning release or liberation, and results in *nirvana.* It is a state of consciousness in which one recognizes his or her status as the ground of all being, i.e., as *Brahman.* It is liberating in that it provides a release from the self-deception and suffering (*dukkha*) of *maya.*

Maya is the universe of conceptual abstractions, the mind's attempt to fit experience into a set of fixed categories. It is the state in which the world is compartmentalized, in which the world is divided into discrete and differentiated objects. It is the condition in which abstractions are mistaken for reality. It is a mental state in which individuals pursue abstract ideals and seek to satisfy their transient desires. Because such desires arise from a fundamental confusion, they can never be satisfied, leaving the individual in a more or less continuous state of *dukkha.*

Maya is immersion in dualism, so that *moksha* is liberation from dualism. Such liberation means an escape from identification with the ego and all other necessarily false notions of the self. When released from such conceptual errors, the mind becomes capable of understanding its true nature as *atman.* Of course, the idea of *atman* is itself a kind of conceptual abstraction, so that it cannot be taken as a goal to be pursued or as a "true" self to be discovered beneath the layers of convention. To put faith in such a self is further entanglement in *maya*.

To exaggerate somewhat, it is the realization that the *atman* cannot successfully be sought after that forms the basis for the Buddha's teaching.

IV

The word "buddha" means enlightened one. Used as a proper name, the phrase "the Buddha" refers to the title afforded the founder of the system of thought bearing this name. Buddhism thus has a twofold meaning, implying both that its adherents are in some sense followers of the Buddha, and that they themselves seek to become a buddha.

The Buddha was a historical figure living in India during the fifth and sixth centuries B.C. His given name was Siddhartha; his family name Gautama. He is also referred to (in the Japanese tradition) as Sakyamuni. Although much of his life is obscured by legend, the general outline is known with some certainty. He was born in what is now Nepal to relatively wealthy and politically powerful parents. At the age of twenty-nine he renounced this life to become a sage (*rishi*) in search of peace, or *moksha*. He wandered for several years, practicing meditation, yoga, asceticism, and other spiritual disciplines. Despite, or perhaps because of, such efforts, he made little progress. Search as he might, the *atman* remained out of reach. One night, while sitting beneath the fabled Bodhi Tree at Gaya, he was enlightened. Following this incident, the remainder of his life was devoted to instructing the many followers he attracted.

The basis of his teaching is contained in what have become known as the Four Noble Truths. As is traditionally understood, Siddhartha's purpose in leading a life of contemplation was to expose the cause of human suffering and, having done so, to specify a remedy. The Four Noble Truths are thus expressed in the manner of a doctor treating a patient, in that they specify the nature of the problem and make suggestions for a cure.

The First of the Truths is the observation that *dukkha* is pervasive in life. As we have seen, *dukkha* is suffering or unhappiness of any kind, but particularly that which comes from our discontent with life. The desire for wealth or respect is *dukkha*. The distaste for bad weather or warm beer is *dukkha*. The fear of death and the passage of time is *dukkha*. In sum, the life of ordinary consciousness is *dukkha*.

The cause of *dukkha*, the Second Truth asserts, is craving or clutching at life (*tanha*). Our unhappiness results from our desiring to make life fit our preconceptions of what it should be or what we would like it to be. The discontent that is *dukkha* is a product of our cravings in the expansive sense of all efforts of the mind to mold experience. *Dukkha* arises when we attempt to fit the world into the dualistic patterns of a conceptual order, i.e., when we are trapped in *maya*.

The Third Truth suggests that *dukkha* can be ended by ending the craving, which can in turn be achieved, per the Fourth Truth, by following the Noble Eightfold Path. The first two steps upon this path relate to the mind: (1) right views, and (2) right understanding. They concern the proper understanding of the Buddha's doctrine or method, and in that sense, render the remainder redundant. They imply that the acolyte appreciate the nature of *dukkha* and the manner in which it arises from *tanha*.

The next three steps refer to action or ethics: (3) right speech, (4) right conduct, and (5) right vocation. Although these bear some resemblance to ethical or moral rules, it is misleading to think of them in such terms. Rather than being strict rules deduced from some transcendent power (such as God) or normative premise (such as Kant's categorical imperative), these are simply suggestions of prudence. They are to be followed not because one has an obligation to observe them, but because doing so is likely to facilitate spiritual achievement. The suggestion is not that there is anything inherently sinful in, say, promiscuity or drunkenness, but only that obsession with such worldly pleasures may stand in the way of enlightenment. In this way, the Buddha's strictures are quite similar in substance to Aristotle's aphorism "all things in moderation."

The three final stages concern meditation: (6) right effort, (7) right awareness (*smriti*), and (8) right contemplation (*samadhi*). While not strictly equivalent, the latter terms do not lend themselves to an easy analytical distinction. *Smriti* implies complete and unlimited awareness, in the sense of perceiving and experiencing all that enters awareness without distorting it. *Tanha* ceases, so that the mind stops its perpetual attempts to clutch at experience. To use the Taoist metaphor, *smriti* is using the mind like a mirror. It is in effect *wu-wei*, the condition in which the mind is passive but clear. It is a state in which dualism is transcended and the ego abandoned.

Samadhi is the resulting frame of mind in which the individual is capable of experiencing reality. It is characterized by peace, meaning the absence of *dukkha*, in that the mind is no longer divided against itself in the form of experience and ego. In the same way, the world is no longer divided into self and environment, thoughts and thinker, black and white. *Samadhi* is a state of contemplation in which time does not exist, the world is not divided into categories, and the mind is at rest. To again invoke an Aristotelian concept, the human *telos* is obtained in *samadhi*.

V

As originally cast, Buddhism differed from its Hindu foundations by carrying forward the logic of dualism in three fundamental ways. First, the Buddha endorsed the twin doctrines of *anatta* and *anicca*. As we have seen, Hindu thought supposed the existence of the higher self, of the *atman*. Siddartha maintained that this self was just another abstraction, and that, as such, was something which stood in the way of true enlightenment. In other words, the *atman* could come to be another concept of the self, which like the ego, would necessarily preclude the end of dualistic thinking. So long as the *atman* was held in the mind as an object of searching, the illusion of *maya* could not be broken. The doctrine of *anatta* (or *anatman*) thus held that the *atman* was itself unreal. Thus the Buddha believed that it was impossible to discover the true self, in that there is no such self (*atman*) to be found. Accordingly, it is sometimes suggested that *atman* is *anatman*, i.e., that the true self is no-self.

The notion of the self, whether ego or *atman*, is thus seen to be an unfortunate conceptual error. No self in the sense of an enduring center of experience can possibly exist, for the same reason that solids simultaneously cannot be liquids. One's identity is illusory, with the self being composed only of the totality of things in awareness. Of course, the things in awareness are constantly in flux, so that in the absence of any identity in the form of ego, or even *atman*, the "self" is itself (in) flux. Hence, the actual self is impermanence or *anicca* (or *anitya*).

Siddartha departed from the Veda in a second important way by stressing the centrality of experience. Wisdom, he said, does not come from scripture, tradition, teachers, gurus, or yogis. Instead, genuine understanding can come only from what is known personally. Because all of our basic ideas (concepts) are socially determined, we cannot be certain about the true nature of reality so long as we continue to think in dualistic patterns. On its face, this contention serves merely to cast doubt upon conventional knowledge, and, as such, is entirely traditional.

Taken seriously, such a position becomes subversive in that it seemingly implies complete philosophical agnosticism. By enshrining personal experience as the requirement

94

for all genuine knowledge, the Buddha reduced all philosophy, like all conventional religion, to vacuous speculation. More generally, he institutionalized doubt to such a degree that it suggests a form of radical skepticism which rejects any truth that is not discovered directly, so that all metaphysical or theological issues become unintelligible. Anticipating the arguments of Bertrand Russell and other logical positivists more than two millennia later, the Buddha regarded such questions as logically and practically meaningless. Questions about life after death, the existence of gods, or the transmigration of souls could not be answered for the reason that they do not express meaningful interrogatories.

Given that fact, the Buddha, in a third departure from the teaching of the Upanishads, rejected a literal interpretation of the Hindu belief in the round of birth and death (*samsara*). Quite clearly, the question of what may happen after death is not subject to personal knowledge, so that any commentary on the fate (or even existence) of the soul is superfluous and foolish. As was his fashion, the Buddha thus declined to discuss or consider such notions. In limiting his attention to the realm of experience, he implicitly argued that reincarnation, guided by the principle of *karma*, be discarded. Instead of the continuing drama of souls led from life to life by the degree and direction of their immersement in life, rebirth occurs from moment to moment in the form of the continuous ego. Thus, I am in a constant process of reincarnation until I am delivered from the round by transcending the ego. This is *nirvana*.

VI

In the centuries following Gautama, there developed a large variety of Buddhist sects. Zen has its origins in one of the later of these schools, the so-called *Mahayana*. While the history of this movement is not well understood, the *Mahayana* appears to have become established by the first

95

century B.C. Rather than a doctrinaire revolution against prevailing monastic practice, it evolved gradually as an attempt to address the many questions that the Buddha's teaching left unanswered.

Buddhist theory suggests that there are a variety of methods or vehicles (*yana*) for achieving *nirvana*. *Mahayana* means the "greater (*maha*) vehicle." It is opposed to the other principal school, which *Mahayana* adherents unabashedly call the "little (*hina*) vehicle." It is the greater vehicle because it alone provides a mechanism for the salvation of all sentient beings via the ideal of the *bodhisattva*. This term denotes an individual who, having achieved full enlightenment and thus the ability to enter *nirvana*, chooses instead to remain in the world so as to assist other living things. The *bodhisattva* is thus a buddha who foregoes release from *samsara* for the sake of helping other creatures attain buddhahood. Other approaches which aim only at self-enlightenment are thought to be selfish, in that they do nothing to relieve the suffering of others. Hence, the *Mahayana* is great, in that it alone fulfills the Buddha's goal of ending the world of *dukkha*.

While the notion of the *bodhisattva* imports a potentially unhealthy emphasis on martyrdom, it does represent an advancement in the logic of Buddhism. If there is no person (ego) who exists, then this person can hardly escape from *samsara*. Accordingly, it makes little sense for one to try to do so. Following the doctrine of *wu-wei*, the attempt to attain *nirvana* is just more intervention against nature. The seeking of release from *samsara* simply breeds greater attachment to the world, in that it feeds the illusion of the person seeking such release. Thus, by pursuing *nirvana* one drives it away by making more *karma*. In this way, it is apparent that the quest for *nirvana* is itself *samsara*.

This is entirely obvious from the concept of *nirvana*. If the state we call *nirvana* is in fact the state of consciousness that results when the mind stops clutching the world, it becomes ridiculous to believe that one can obtain *nirvana* by clutching at life. Put differently, *nirvana* is the condition of the mind in which it has stopped trying to control or understand the world. It is a situation in which the conscious mind has ceased all striving, i.e., all efforts to interfere with the stream of experience. To try to flee from *samsara* is such interference, so that by definition the campaign directed toward *nirvana* is *samsara*. In other words, entrapment in *samsara* is precisely one's attempts to leave it.

It follows, then, that one's natural, uncontrolled stream of experience is itself *nirvana*. One moves away from *nirvana* by attempting to cease this line of experience and artificially enthrone some new, arbitrary ideal of better, or more perfect, experience. Because *nirvana* is the absence of desire, it cannot be found by desiring it, for you cannot desire to stop desiring. *Nirvana* is thus to be obtained by abandoning all attempts to reach it. This leads inescapably to the fundamental realization that *samsara* is *nirvana*.

From this perspective, we see what appears (on the surface at least) to be an inconsistency or contradiction within the *Tao*. If, as has been suggested, "all is the *Tao*," then surely failure to appreciate this fact is also the *Tao*. Hence, in not seeing the *Tao*, I am already living by the *Tao*, so that by not being "in the *Tao*," I am, in fact, "in the *Tao*." In the same way, the artificialities of convention are themselves natural, inherent in the nature of our ability to reason, so that in following convention I am in fact acting in accordance with *te*.

It is thus unnecessary, indeed, counter-productive, to attempt to become a buddha, in that one is already a buddha. In terms of the *Tao*, there is no need to follow it, in that one has no other choice. There is no need to seek liberation, in that you are already free. Enlightenment or liberation, then, cannot be obtained by conscious effort, in that they are already possessed. The end point of liberation

97

is thus not in leaving *samsara*, but in realizing that you were never there.

Seen in this light, the world of convention is not something to be scorned or renounced, and the *bodhisattva* does no such thing. In a literal sense, the *bodhisattva* thus does not choose to renounce deliverance into *nirvana*, in that there is no *nirvana* to be delivered into, nor any person to make such a choice. Instead, the bodhisattva realizes the futility, even the folly, of imagining a *nirvana* distinct from day-to-day life as normally understood. *Mahayana* doctrine goes on to suggest that this insight fosters compassion, so that the *bodhisattva* is moved to concern for human suffering. However, such a conceit is unnecessary, in that having made the discovery, an individual would spontaneously—precisely through not acting or *wu-wei*—share it with others.

The *bodhisattva* ideal aside, the question remains as to how one manages to stop desiring. How, in other words, do you follow a way of liberation without seeking liberation? An answer of sorts is provided by Nagarjuna (third century A.D.), the principal theorist of the *Mahayana* school, in the so-called doctrine of emptiness (*Sunyata*). In much the same way as the Taoists, Nagarjuna holds that "all is void," in the sense that our mental constructs of the world are without substance. In effect, he questions all dualistic distinctions, and thus all our ideas about life and reality.

Sunyata is thus a process of denying the reality of everything, or rather, of all abstractions and arguments that build upon them. It suggests that objects, ideas, places, events—anything that could be expressed by nouns, verbs, adjectives, and adverbs—are illusions of the mind. All ideas, such as those of peace or happiness, *maya* and *Brahman*, *dukkha* and *moksha*, *nirvana* and *samsara*, are to be dismissed as nonsense. All theories, all propositions—in sum—all speculation is to be denounced as evidence of a diseased mind. By negation, one demonstrates the uselessness and absurdity of everything. *Sunyata* thus maintains that reality is empty, or rather that by definition all human attempts to categorize, explain, or otherwise grasp reality are empty. By negation, we deny the validity of all ideas, so as to reduce the mind to the clarity of the mirror suggested by Chuang-tzu.

To reiterate, the dualistic map we superimpose over matter and experience is an empty phantasm that is inherently and inescapably unreal. All our words and concepts, including those of our own desires and thoughts, are delusions. Accordingly, there is nothing to grasp or pursue. Thus, to return to the problem at hand, you cannot seek *nirvana*, in that there is no *nirvana* to seek. When this fact is realized, it becomes painfully apparent that in struggling with the self to become a buddha, the aspirant has been wrestling with a ghost. There is no self to be rid of, no buddha to be found. All your efforts are in vain, in that ultimately you cannot find anything, in that nothing exists.

Though it plainly implies that there are no truths or things of value, *Sunyata* is not a form of nihilism. The purpose of negation is not an end in itself, but only a means to the realization that reality lies beyond dualistic descriptions. To see reality directly, to experience without the convolutions of abstractions, it is necessary to eliminate abstractions. It is not that nothing remains after negation, in that negation exposes reality. To borrow an example from Suzuki, the proper answer to the question of what remains of life when everything is denied is a slap in the face.[6] The experience of being slapped is real enough—it remains. What is denied is the idea of being slapped, the labelling of the experience, the attempt to reduce the experience into an icy, lifeless abstraction. The negation of dualism, then, is really an affirmation of experience.

Sunyata thus aims not at leaving the mind vacuous, as critics of Zen have suggested, but at allowing it to be filled with experience. Negation cleans or polishes the mirror, rather than breaking it or coloring it black. By denying everything, Buddhism does not deny the world, but only our ideas about the world. In the same way, Buddhism is not (as is sometimes argued) "anti-life" because it is anti-dualistic. Instead, it endorses life precisely by opposing all ideas about life. From this perspective, the very core of *Sunyata* is the affirmation of life, in that it is the fact that life is valued which leads to the negation of abstractions which lessen our capacity to live it.

When we rid life of abstractions, we are in the emptiness of the void. Yet the world does not vanish; matter continues to exist and the mind continues to function. What has happened is that we have ceased imposing form or structure, so that experience is no longer divided into dualistic categories. Trees, planets, light, colors, books, and all other conceptual categories are seen to be devoid of meaning. By denying these things, the process of negation tells us what the world is not, leaving us with whatever it is. We replace the universe of the mind's mental constructs, the world seen through the lenses of abstraction, with things as they really are. The literature (as previously mentioned) sometimes uses the Sanskrit construction *tathata*, meaning "thatness" or "suchness" to refer to the world when it is seen in this way. In a strict sense, the word is logically meaningless, but its use suggests the concrete rather than the abstract, experience rather than ideas about experience. It is the "stuff" of reality when it is not divided, categorized, or otherwise dualistically "processed" by the mind.

VII

Zen arose as a distinct movement or sect within the *Mahayana* school as Buddhist monks encountered Taoist and neo-Taoist ideas as they brought Buddhism to China in the early centuries of the first millennium A.D. The advent of Zen was a synthesis of *Mahayana* doctrine with the Taoist emphasis on simplicity, naturalness, spontaneity, and the intellectual pacifism of *wu-wei*. For the sake of brevity and relevance, we will forego an account of this process, turning our attention instead to the first manifestations of Zen.[7]

The first identifiable strand of Zen can be found in the writings of Tao-sheng (360 – 434), who argued that enlightenment can only be obtained spontaneously. While in some readings the Buddhist scriptures superficially suggested such a position, they also seemed to imply that *nirvana* could only come about as the unfolding of a process. As the individual learned to let go of life, he or she would slowly loosen the hold of *karma*. Tao-sheng observes that if *nirvana* cannot be acquired by questing after it, then it can hardly be found gradually. To progress toward awakening (*bodhi*) like one climbing a stair of spiritual attainment is to imply that such awakening is just something else to be had. By so doing, he makes the first well-articulated case for sudden enlightenment. This position would become axiomatic to Zen, so that some scholars regard him as the founder of Zen.[8]

The traditionally recognized "first patriarch of Zen" is the monk Bodhidharma, who is said to have arrived in China sometime after 450 A.D. It is unclear whether he was a historical figure, though Japanese scholars widely believe that he was. In any case, he is universally regarded as second in importance only to the Buddha himself in the history of Zen. In four well-known lines of verse, credited to him but apparently written much later, a convenient summary of Zen is articulated:[9]

> A special transmission outside the scriptures
> Not founded upon words and letters;
> By pointing directly to the mind
> It lets one see into nature and thus attain
> Buddhahood.

Line one is subject to two (not mutually exclusive) interpretations. The more conventional relates the "special transmission" to the almost certainly false (but officially sanctioned) contention that Zen derived from a direct "transmission" from the Buddha to his disciple Mahakasyapa (sometimes just Kasyapa). In this way, the Buddha entrusted his teaching to Mahakasyapa, thus implying a special endorsement of the Zen school. Bodhidharma, in turn, was the twenty-eighth descendant of that transmission. The story is legendary rather than factual, but it long served as a useful justification for Zen's odd claim to be the (one) true manifestation of Buddhism.

In the second, equally valid, interpretation, the critical phrase becomes "outside the scriptures," sometimes translated as "outside tradition," with the meaning that the transmission of enlightenment does not depend upon (or is beyond) the Buddhist tradition and its associated methods.

This latter meaning is similar to the second line, which implies that Zen is not to be found in the words or contrivances of philosophy or systematization. Instead, as Tao-shen reminds us, enlightenment must occur spontaneously. As dualistic artifacts of the mind, words are insufficient guides toward *nirvana*. Instead, as line three makes clear, the proper path is shown by "direct pointing." Thus, Zen teaching does not rely upon words or symbols of any type. Rather than producing a doctrine or philosophy to explain itself, Zen acts directly. As a method of instruction, Zen "points" to the world of *tathata* instead of weaving a net of words. By so doing, the disguise of reality is removed (line four).

The emphasis upon direct pointing institutionalized an enigmatic form of teaching based upon the telling of parables (*mondo*). Virtually all of the classical Zen literature consists of these anecdotes, for the most part designed to provoke a deeper understanding in a direct rather than symbolic fashion. As Alan Watts explains, *mondo*[10] cannot be "explained" without spoiling their effect. In some respects they are like jokes which do not produce their intended effect of laughter when the "punch line" requires further explanation. One must see the point immediately, or not at all.

One invariably encounters two such anecdotes in discussions of Bodhidharma. The first, expressed as a koan in the collection called the *Mumonkan*, begins with the monk Hui-k'o repeatedly asking Bodhidharma for instruction. Reluctantly, the latter finally relents and asks Hui-k'o what it is he wants.

> "Your disciple's mind is not yet at peace. I beg you, my teacher, please give it peace."

> Bodhidharma said, "Bring your mind to me and I will set it at rest."

> Hui-k'o replied, "I have searched for my mind, but I cannot find it."

> Bodhidharma said, "Then I have thoroughly set it at peace for you."

As in most koans, this one ends with Hui-k'o being awakened upon the teacher's answer. In the second *mondo*, a koan from the *Hekiganroku* nicely illustrating *Sunyata*, such enlightenment does not result. Bodhidharma is conversing with the Emperor Wu when the latter asks what merit (or spiritual progress) he has gained from his efforts in building temples, translating sutras, and otherwise promoting Buddhism.

> Bodhidharma replied, "No merit at all."

> Perplexed, the Emperor asked, "What, then, is the sacred truth's first principle?"

> Bodhidharma answered, "Vast emptiness, nothing sacred."

Angered, the Emperor demanded, "Who is it that faces me?"

Bodhidharma said, "I don't know."

"Direct pointing" also refers to meditation. The way to "the mind" (i.e., *satori*) is not through symbols and words, but through the experience of reality that occurs when the mind stops clutching the world. Meditation, the argument continues, is the key toward the end of such clutching. For this reason, Zen is often described as the *dhyana* (or meditational) school of *Mahayana* Buddhism.[11] The stress on meditation is evident in another of Bodhidharma's legendary exploits, in which he is said to have remained in seated meditation (zazen) for nine years, staring at the same wall until his legs withered into dust. This was his method of liberation: unending contemplation through "wall gazing" until salvation was found. The centrality of meditative practice is seen throughout the teachings of Bodhidharma's successors. In a typical remark, Tao-hsin, the third successor and thus "fourth partriarch," constantly reminded his followers that "sitting in meditation is basic to all else." It is this, more than anything else, that became the legacy of Bodhidharma.

The last major step in the establishment of Zen occurred under Hui-neng (638 – 713), the sixth patriarch. Another much revered figure, he is widely regarded as establishing Zen in something approximating its current form. As with Bodhidharma, Hui-neng is credited with a re-interpretation of existing Buddhist theory. The point of departure in his teaching is fixed around an incident when he was a student under Hung-jan, the fifth patriarch. Hung-jan was preparing to select a successor and announced a competition in which the monks were asked to submit a short stanza illustrating their understanding of Zen. The elder monk and heir-apparent wrote the following:[12]

> The body is the Bodhi-tree;
> The soul is like the mirror bright;
> Take heed to keep it always clean,
> And let no dust collect upon it.

Such lines nicely summarized the then dominant view of meditational practice.[13] As the familiar metaphor of the mirror suggests, the mind is held to be kept "clean" by preventing thoughts ("dust") from accumulating on it. As a method for maintaining such cleanliness, meditation is viewed as a process of concentrating—staring at Bodhidharma's wall—so as to eliminate all thoughts or desires.

In reply, Hui-neng proposed alternative lines running thus:

> The Bodhi is not like the tree;
> The mirror bright is no where shining:
> As there is nothing from the first,
> Where does the dust collect itself?

Hui-neng thus rejects the analogy of mind to mirror, in that the former cannot be held by the mind as an object of awareness or understanding. To suggest otherwise is to reduce the mind to another abstraction. As the above lines express, just as there are really no such things as mirrors (or dust for that matter), there are no minds.

The absence of the mind as a conceptual category implies that it cannot be "controlled," in that something which does not exist can hardly be controlled. Given that the mind cannot be controlled by your will or effort, how can you possibly keep it clean? Put another way, the very effort of cleaning the mind is an act of dirtying it. The idea of cleansing the mind is thus contradictory and self-frustrating. Given the imperative of *wu-wei*, it is clear that you are not in fact being spontaneous by the artificial, contrived effort at keeping the mind a spotless mirror. As Shen-hui nicely puts it, "If working with the mind is to discipline one's mind, how could this be called deliverance?"

105

The idea of the mind as something to be laundered, or otherwise consciously controlled, is a further endorsement for naturalness. Meditation does not mean an abandonment of your humanity by reducing the mind to nothingness. Instead, it means letting things happen without the oppression of convention. Thoughts, like the mind itself, are to be "let go of," in the sense that one should neither cling to them nor repress them. To do otherwise is to intervene, contra *wu-wei*. In this way, Hui-neng compares the mind not to a void, but to space. The former is simply empty, while the latter is the arena in which things take place. The mind-as-space, then, is a vision of the mind in which thoughts and perceptions come and go, like planets moving through the heavens.

The phrase "the true mind is no mind" is attributed to Hui-neng. It means that the original or natural mind—in effect, the buddha nature—is neither an abstraction nor an object of consciousness. By calling the mind "no-mind" he implies that the mind is not equivalent to any idea about it, so that it cannot be sought after or otherwise attained. His successors pursued this argument further by asserting the entirely obvious conclusion that Zen practice is not a practice at all, in that to practice some discipline implies that one does it for the sake of some achievement. In the same way, they re-affirmed the *Mahayana* conviction that one cannot become a buddha by intending or desiring to be one, in that the very act of intending makes success impossible. Abandoning such a course results in something very much like the ideal state espoused by the Taoists: an unaffected naturalness, in which all self-consciousness has been abandoned.

It is in this spirit that Po-chang (720 – 814) would later define Zen as the advice "When hungry, eat; when tired, sleep." Similarly, Lin-chi (Japanese, Rinzai, ninth century) admonished his students "Just be ordinary and nothing special. Relieve your bowels, pass water, put on your clothes, eat your food. When you are tired, go and lie down." The point is that in its "direct pointing" Zen does not endorse some radical departure from ordinary life. Spirituality is not something foreign to day-to-day life, nor something to be found outside of it. The Absolute, the ground of being, the goal of spirituality, is to be found in the seemingly most mundane, uninteresting, even trivial things: putting on clothes, eating food, passing water.

By the close of the first millennium A.D., then, a reasonably concise picture of Zen as a variant of Buddhism had begun to emerge. It stressed instantaneous enlightenment (*satori*) as opposed to attainment in stages. It opposed the more traditional Indian (and in some ways, Taoist) notion of meditation as the process of clearing the mind of all thoughts. It denied the reality of all dualistic distinctions, including those between *nirvana* and *samsara*, or buddhahood and the ordinary mind. It asserted that we should cultivate naturalness and spontaneity by non-action (*wu-wei*). It maintained that awakening (*bodhi*) is not something to be found, but something to be realized.

As we have seen, most (or all) of these ideas were already present—explicitly or otherwise—in Taoism and pre-Zen *Mahayana* Buddhism. In stark, and perhaps unfair, terms, Zen developed as a successively more encompassing attempt to not only synthesize such notions, but to take them seriously. For this reason it might be said that Zen is the distillation of much of Eastern philosophy, in that it has extracted the final essence from ideas common in the Eastern world.

VII

Modern Japanese Zen consists of two sects, Rinzai and Soto. Both trace their origins to Hui-neng's immediate disciplines; both were effectively systematized and transferred to Japan by approximately 1200. The Zen of Hui-neng and his successors during the T'ang period (ending *c.* 900) was centered solely upon the attainment of satori through personal experience. Given that emphasis, there was neither room nor need for theory or doctrine. The "crisis of Zen" during the subsequent Sung period resulted from the dissipation of the energy of the "old masters" of the T'ang dynasty at the very time when the Zen school was attracting unprecedented numbers of followers. The advent of identifiable schools with decidedly doctrinaire approaches to the study of Zen was thus a conscious reaction to a simultaneous decline in spiritual dynamism and a remarkable explosion of popularity.

For both Rinzai and Soto the core of the method is sitting meditation (*zazen*), a subject which we will discuss in some length in the following chapter. For the moment, it is enough to note that *zazen* is simply sitting, eyes open and fixed on a spot on a wall in front of you. Individuals so engaged are doing nothing more than observing the universe, including their own thoughts, without comment. While it may seem rather unnatural to sit in a single spot for hours on end, this practice is perfectly consistent with Zen "theory" when it is observed that Zen suggests experiencing reality directly. The state of consciousness associated with Zen is thus one in which dualistic distinctions are dropped, so that the mind ceases its clutching at experience. Clearly, this is best accomplished by quietude—by simply being aware of whatever is happening. To use a cliche, *zazen* is the attempt to "live in the now" while simultaneously eliminating the person who is doing this living.

Accordingly, one sits solely for the sake of doing so; sitting has no other purpose. To do *zazen* with some goal in mind, to do it for some particular reason, such as becoming a buddha, is to miss the point entirely. When not trying to fit the world into our conceptual order, when not trying to experience experience, when not consumed with the illusion of the ego, there is simply nothing else to be done. In other words, monks sit because, having seen to other responsibilities, there is no reason to do anything else. This is the essence of *wu-wei*.

A second method, the *koan*, is also used by both Soto and Rinzai, though the latter puts far greater stress (and faith) upon it. The word literally means "public document," though it is often translated as "problem." The latter is closer to the mark idiomatically, in that it suggests the actual usage of the term. The *koan* is a story or anecdote of some type, often in the form of a dialogue between a master and student, or a question followed by an answer. Each *koan* contains in it some insight into Zen which the student is expected to grasp.

The *koan* is often "studied" in conjunction with *zazen*, so that the two practices merge. Its *raison d'etre* is identical to that of *zazen* alone: to lead the student to *satori*. Meditation seems a more natural expression of Zen, in that the practice of *zazen* is itself an obvious form of Zen. In this way, Zen-as-method becomes identical with Zen-as-end. The *koan* is more artificial, and because of this it seems to lend itself to the same mistake in regard to *satori* that the Buddha saw in the *atman*: by making it an object of pursuit, we reduce it to another abstraction which cannot be obtained.

The method is also sometimes assailed for its alleged resemblance to catechism or confirmation classes. There are grades of achievement which acolytes must pass by providing satisfactory answers to several *koans* of varying levels of difficulty. Those who complete the entire, very long course, earn the title *roshi* (or master), and are thus empowered to offer instruction to others, much like the Ph.D. entitles one to teach undergraduates. The difficulty in this approach is that it suggests the entirely odd notion that there are different levels of *satori*, that other people are qualified to judge one's level of attainment, and that final enlightenment can be approached piecemeal, in the manner that one learns to master mathematics or horseback riding.

109

In spite of these difficulties, the *koan* system has many adherents. It is often defended on the grounds that, its unnaturalness aside, it (in conjunction with *zazen*) has proven itself remarkably useful in leading the individual to understanding. Given that such a claim is made most loudly by the class of individuals—the *roshi*—who have an obvious personal stake in perpetuating current practice, it should be taken with the proverbial healthy dose of salt.

Having said that, it is nonetheless difficult to argue with the proposition that the *koan*, like other artificialities such as antibiotics or aspirin, can be of enormous value. Just as a commitment to Zen does not imply one should die of pneumonia because of a refusal to take penicillin, it does not suggest that one forego unnatural exercises like the *koan* only because they are unnatural. Like all products of human ingenuity, the *koan* is a legitimate instrument so long as it is seen for the contrivance that it is.

The *koan* exists to hammer upon the walls of logic and convention until they collapse. The basic premise is to confront the student with a story or question which is utterly incomprehensible. Viewed from the perspective of ordinary consciousness fixed upon dualistic thinking, the *koan* is nothing more than mindless gibberish. It is this very absurdity that opens the mind, that slowly evokes the possibility of doubting the world of dualism. In other words, the *koan* is like an attorney cross-examining a witness. By constant questioning, even badgering, the questioner begins to expose the basic contradictions of the witness's position. Finally, the level of doubt about this position reaches a critical level and the entire edifice collapses. By employment of the *koan*, the *roshi* leads the student to a similar collapse of faith. As Heinrich Dumoulin explains it,[14]

> The essence of the *koan* is to be rationally unresolvable and thus to point to what is arational. The *koan* urges us to abandon our rational thought structures

and step beyond our usual state of consciousness in order to press into new and unknown dimensions.

In his oft-quoted foreword to Suzuki's influential introduction to Zen, Carl Jung has explained this process in terms of the Freudian division of the mind into conscious and unconscious.[15] In his view, *satori* is, in effect, the liberation of the unconscious, an event that allows it to join the conscious mind in a holistic unity. The *koan* induces this marriage by straining the psyche to such a degree that the ordinarily irreconcilable division of the self fuses together. Loosely put, by rendering the mind whole, the ego and other dualistic distinctions fall away, leaving the "natural" mind.

Theory aside, the nature of the *koan* exercise is best explained through example. A common problem given to beginning students, the best known of all *koans*, is the so-called "Joshu's *Mu*." The student is asked to explain why the monk Joshu (in Chinese, Chao-Chao) answered no (*mu*) to the question "Does a dog have the buddha nature?" It is axiomatic to all schools of the *Mahayana* that all sentient beings have the buddha nature, so that to respond "no" is equivalent to asserting that "2 + 2 = 5."

Other *koans* involve answers to the traditional question of the significance of Bodhidharma's arrival from the East (i.e., from India), which is equivalent to asking "What is the fundamental principle of Buddhism?" A typical answer, again attributed to Joshu, is "The cypress tree in the garden." To the similar question of "What is the Buddha," T'ung-shan responded "Three pounds of flax."

Although these answers seem paradoxical, there are reasonably obvious rationalizations for such replies. In the first, it appears that Joshu was trying to dislodge the complacency of his students by saying something outrageous. By denying well established doctrine, Joshu sought to illustrate that all reliance on convention of any type, including the *Mahayana*, is foolish. In the second, the puzzling comments about trees and flax seem to be attempts to focus the mind away from idle theorizing about Buddhism and back toward the concrete world of reality that is the true subject of the Buddha's teaching.

While these answers have some plausibility, and are in a sense perfectly correct, they represent precisely the sort of analysis the *roshi* wants to banish. When the student understands the parable only in the limited sense of conceptualization, the value of the exercise is completely lost. By realizing that Joshu is attempting to focus your attention on existence rather than speculation, you are still engaging in speculation. In feeling clever over seeing through the apparent inanity of "three pounds of flax," you have missed the point. If anything, the ease with which these examples lend themselves to conceptual, rational answers is a purposeful trap set for the over-eager student.

This is made clear in a *mondo* regarding Fa-yen and his student Hsuan-tzu. The former inquired as to why the latter did not ask questions, to which the latter replied that he had already been instructed by an earlier teacher. When asked to explain, Hsuan-tzu said that in reply to the standard query "What is the Buddha?" this master had said "Ping-ting comes for fire!" Fa-yen agreed that this was an excellent answer, but challenged the student to explain it. Hsuan-tzu replied that Ping-ting is the god of fire, so that for him to seek for fire is to seek for something he already possesses. In the same way, he continued, there is no need to seek the Buddha, in that one is the Buddha already. Fa-yen laughed, saying, "Just as I thought, you do not understand."

Every time one thinks a problem is solved by some answer like the one Hsuan-tzu accepted, the *roshi* will not be satisfied. This process will continue, often for months or years, until the disciple realizes that there is no symbolic or allegorical answer, no truth hidden behind the nonsense. When this is finally and fully understood, it becomes appar-

112

ent that the entire mode of analysis, the asking of a conventional question and a conventional (though irrational) answer is meaningless. In turn, it is seen that the effort of fitting the world into abstractions is the necessarily impossible attempt of the mind to experience the process of experience. The *koan* is solved when the mind becomes so thoroughly exhausted from its efforts to do just this that it surrenders. To struggle in this way is to pit the unmovable object of the *koan* against the irresistible force of reason. The conflict ends when the latter is seen to be illusory.

One peers into the "meaning" of the *koan* when it becomes readily apparent that the *koan* is an empty trap of logic which is solvable only by experiencing its vacuity. By so doing, one comes to understand the *koan* in the same way one knows how to hear or breathe. While you could explain the general process by which a person, in the abstract, does these things, you cannot possibly express the manner in which you cause these things to be done, in that they are not something you do. Instead, these things are you. The attempt to see beyond experience to the person who has experience (the ego) is seen as the logical equivalent of the *koan*.

For this reason, it has been suggested that we study the *koan* because the *koan* is the self, by which is meant that the self-as-ego is another of these logical pitfalls that causes enormous pain until we see it for what it is. As the discomfort of the *koan* disappears when one sees through it, so the discomfort of life dissipates when we see through the conceptual error known as the ego. A *koan* points toward our true selves, i.e., toward the buddha nature, because it has no symbolic or conceptual meaning. The *koan* does not point to anything else; it simply is. In the same way, the true self represents or stands for nothing else. Just as the *koan* is "empty" in the sense that it contains nothing that can be expressed or understood in terms of abstractions, so is the buddha nature. Above all else, this is the fundamental

113

"conclusion" of Zen: your life does not represent or stand for anything. As we saw in the preceding chapter, your life has no "meaning" in terms of words or ideas. The affinity of the *koan* and the self is apparent given that the *koan* also has no meaning in these terms. Life, like the *koan*, cannot be explained in terms of anything else.

Seen in this light, the institutionalization of the *koan* has definite commendatory properties. When viewed as a kind of trudgeon for beating down the confining walls of convention, *koan* training (as well as *zazen*) becomes a valuable means to enlightenment. Unfortunately, it is all too often the case that the means become mistaken for the end, so that the *koan* becomes synonymous with the study of Zen, or even Zen itself.

Nowhere is this tunnel vision more clearly seen than in the smug superiority of Rinzai "fundamentalists" who dismiss as revisionist heresies any attempts to explain or practice Zen outside of the Nipponese tradition. As their example makes clear, it is imperative to resist the temptation of systematizing Zen by reducing it to a rigorous orthodoxy. As the old masters remind us, one does not become a buddha by meditating, solving *koans*, or following any other method. To enshrine a particular cultural vision of Zen as an ideal for others to follow is a peculiar attachment to the very ego such methods endeavor to vanquish.

114

NOTES

1. For a general discussion of Taoism, see K. Bhaskra Rao, *Taoism and Buddhism* (Vijawada, India: Navodaya Publishers, 1971). A less scholarly and rather more personal account is J.C. Cooper, *Taoism: The Way of the Mystic* (Kent, U.K.: The Aquarian Press, 1990).
2. Lao-tzu argues that one of the principle virtues flowing from the *Tao* is weakness rather than strength, pacificism rather than aggression. This is inherent in the ideal of action through non-action (*wu-wei*). The *Tao-te Ching* thus provides what may be the first well-articulated argument for pacifism, as well as the first extant admonition to return evil with good. It is for this reason that Taoism is often interpreted as much as a political doctrine as a metaphysical one.
3. H. Giles, *Taoist Teachings* (London: Murray, 1925).
4. As an example, the mental uncertainty of "deliberation" is interference with the mind in the sense that we second-guess our initial, spontaneous, natural decisions.
5. *The Papers of Thomas Jefferson*, Edward Dumbauld, ed., (Indianapolis: Bobbs-Merrill, 1955) vol. 12, p. 15.
6. D.T. Suzuki, *An Introduction to Zen Buddhism* (New York: Grove Press, 1964).
7. For a readable discussion of these developments, and the general history of early Zen, see Heinrich Dumoulin's definitive *Zen Buddhism: A History (India and China)* (New York: Macmillan, 1988).
8. For a brief account, see Dumoulin, *Zen Buddhism: A History (India and China)*, chapter 5.
9. For a discussion, see Dumoulin, *Zen Buddhism: A History (India and China)*, chapter 5.
10. Alan Watts, *The Way of Zen* (New York: Vintage, 1989), p. 87.

11. This is explicit in the etymology of "zen," given that the word comes from the Chinese *ch'an*, which is itself a transliteration of the Sanskrit *dhyana*, meaning meditation.

12. Wong Mou-Lam, *The Sutra of Wei Lang (Hui-neng)* (London: Luzac, 1944).

13. In essence, such a view continues to be prevalent in much of contemporary Hindu, (non-Zen) Buddhist, and Taoist practice.

14. Dumoulin, *Zen Buddhism: A History (India and China)*, p. 246.

15. In Suzuki, *An Introduction to Zen Buddhism.*

CHAPTER SIX

Meditation and the Practice of Zen

How could sitting in meditation make a Buddha?
        —Haui-jang

How, by practicing samadhi, *could one attain*
samadhi?
        —Shen-hui

Zen is conventionally thought of as the *dhyana* or meditation school of Buddhism, yet meditation is central to virtually all Buddhist sects. To appreciate what differentiates the practice of meditation in Zen from other Buddhist schools, return to the account of the succession of the fourth patriarch, Hui-jang. Recall the distinction between Hui-neng's poem and that of the other candidate who described the mind as an entity which, much like a mirror, is to be kept "clean" by preventing thoughts ("dust") from accumulating upon it. In the mirror metaphor, meditation is practiced as a means to the end of eliminating all thoughts and desires. To meditate is thus to focus concentration on some fixed point, so as to drive out the "distractions" that result from one's environment and one's own mind. In this approach, meditation is the process of calming the mind by driving out all cognition and perception.

Hui-neng confounded this view by negating the dualistic distinctions implicit in it:[1]

There never was a Bodhi Tree,
Nor bright mirror standing.
Fundamentally, not one thing exists,
So where is the dust to cling?

This distinction and all that it implies is fundamental to Zen meditation. In Zen, the mind is not to be controlled or transformed by meditation into an empty consciousness devoid of stimuli. Rather, the true experience of "no-mind" is exactly that—a state of consciousness where one is not conscious of having a mind. There is no imperative to concentrate so as to erase or cleanse the mind, because the very act of trying to "clean" the mind is to "dirty" it.

One cannot work on the mind with the mind, in the sense that one cannot consciously desire to cease conscious desiring. The true mind is "no-mind," uncontrolled and controlled, unchanneled and channeled, completely aware of the now, not of itself. Put differently, the mind, like the self, is a conceptual abstraction, so that any attempt to focus concentration in an effort to be rid of the mind is to continue to be trapped within an illusion. Rather than exerting effort, we follow *wu-wei* so as to experience whatever it is we are experiencing without reliance on abstractions. As Hui-neng says,

> Thoughts come and go of themselves, for through the use of wisdom there is not blockage.

Alternatively:

> To concentrate on the mind and to contemplate it until it is still is a disease and not *dhyana*.

And again:

> If you start concentrating the mind on stillness, you will merely produce an unreal stillness. . . . What does the word "meditation" mean? In this school it means no barriers, no obstacles; it is beyond all objective situations whether good or bad. The word "sitting" means not to stir up thoughts in the mind.

Of course, one can only come to see this by meditating. When sitting in meditation, the contents of the mind become just other things to be aware of, so that one observes thoughts and emotions as they occur, as if from a distance. Eventually, and paradoxically, one begins to realize that the mind cannot possibly observe itself, in that there is no mind aside from experience, no vantage point from which to see

120

the self. Put differently, we learn to disentangle ourselves from *maya* by experiencing the silence ("no-mind") within the noise (of the mind). The mind's internal chatter, its thoroughly redundant attempt to talk to itself, slowly begins to subside, in that it becomes apparent that there is no one to talk to.

This silence is not to be confused with withdrawal. To rid the mind of this talk is not to be numb or catatonic. Instead, silence is the experience of the present moment, i.e., of reality. In this way, much of life becomes a form of meditation, in that one does not need mental chatter to laugh, to walk, or to eat. In its most expansive sense, meditation can subsume any activity from drinking coffee to washing dishes.

In this context, recall the final stages of the Buddha's Eightfold Path. Collectively, these create awareness and allow such awareness to be experienced without the intervention of one who experiences. In so doing, the self becomes nothing more than experience or awareness. These stages are states that are experienced through the process of becoming fully aware. Right mindfulness concerns the present "momentness" and spontaneity of your life, the experience of the here and now of existence. When tying your shoes, be fully involved in tying your shoes. When talking to a friend, be totally engrossed in the conversation. Correct mindfulness is thus awareness of and absorption in one's experience. It is the state in which attention is focused such that one is not distracted with thoughts of the future or past, right or wrong, pleasant or unpleasant. It is a natural openness which allows access to the experience of reality, i.e., to *samadhi*.

In *samadhi*, one is completely involved or absorbed with life rather than ideas about life. One is thus not concentrating on meditating or holding off thoughts. One is not thinking about experiencing the now or about contemplation. All forms of self-consciousness dissipate, leaving only what is real. In this way, *samadhi* is the logical extension of *satori*, in that the former is the continuing experience of the truth made evident by the latter.

Of course, one does not meditate to achieve *samadhi*, in that the very act of consciously seeking reality makes it impossible to find. If right mindfulness is necessary for *samadhi*, it is plain that one cannot meditate for any reason, in that performing an act for some future goal is to imply a lack of awareness of the here and now. If one sits in meditation so as to become enlightened, part of the mind is necessarily engaged in pursuing such a goal. If so, then meditating for this or any other reason is contrary to the entire enterprise.

Put slightly differently, to meditate with any sort of goal is to impose an artificial structure on experience, whereby one continues to cling to a dualistic notion of enlightenment. So long as there remains a commitment to finding something through meditation, one is implicitly endorsing the notion that there is someone to become enlightened, and that enlightenment can be differentiated from ordinary consciousness. For this reason one does not meditate to become a buddha; one just meditates.

From this perspective, one does not meditate to find *satori*, to achieve communion with God, or to blot out the external world. Instead, one simply contemplates whatever happens to be in awareness. The meditator does not go inside the "self" to effect internal change in order to adjust to the external, in that the boundary between the one contemplating and the things contemplated—that is, between the external and the internal—is illusory. If *satori* consists of the dissolution of this distinction, meditation realizes this state by frustrating the "I," the ego, which maintains boundaries. The paradox is that to attempt purposely to erase these distinctions is to feed the illusion that perpetuates them, so that to consciously strive for enlightenment is to fortify the very boundaries that one is trying to destroy.

II

The distinctive form of meditation within Zen is *zazen*, literally meaning "seated meditation." Its essence is easily described. One sits, traditionally in the lotus posture, eyes open, staring straight head. There is nothing more to it than that. As Dogen admonished, "just sit!"

To practice *zazen* is to be aware of whatever is happening. It is to experience the totality of one's awareness without comment or judgement, without approval or disapproval. Implicit in the "theory" of *zazen* is the notion that a perfect state of such awareness can be attained simply by sitting long enough. Thus, meditation becomes not only a method but an end as well, in that Zen is only and precisely awareness that is not dependent upon dualistic distinctions. By sitting, we slowly begin to tear down the patterns of dualistic thinking, so that ultimately we are left with Zen. For this reason, it is often suggested (with some overstatement) that the practice of *zazen* is Zen itself.

Zen teaching places considerable stress upon posture. Being awake, alert, and having the body's center of balance in a supported position helps prevent the distractions of pain or discomfort. Hence, one is encouraged to sit upright, back straight, legs crossed, in that this position appears to minimize discomfort. There is nothing magical about this "lotus posture." It is not a religious ritual of any kind, nor is it strictly necessary for *zazen*. It is traditionally observed only because it seems to work. To be sure, physical pain may still occur in this posture, but it is neither courted for its own sake nor aggressively avoided; it is simply experienced and accepted.

To begin, a traditional lotus position should be assumed. That is, sitting upright on the floor or a cushion with the legs folded over one another, each foot resting upon the opposite thigh. If this leg position is impossible to attain or is excessively uncomfortable, one may use the half-lotus position: one leg bent and rested on the floor, the other foot resting upon the opposite leg's thigh. The arms are held at the sides without tension in the shoulders, hands are laid in the lap with one open hand holding the back of the other, thumbs touching. The anchor of this position is the spine, which should be kept straight yet supple with the head held at a relaxed, somewhat forward-tilting position. The focus of balance of the body should be kept in the seat and the midsection; this grounds the body and lessens the possibility of strain or tension developing in the back and shoulders.

While one's initial instinct is to close the eyes so as to eliminate distractions, it is these distractions that are the stuff of reality. One's purpose is thus not to shut out sensory data but to experience it. Rather than fixing concentration on a single point, we are trying to eliminate all self-consciousness, including that of concentrating. For this reason, *zazen* is generally done with eyes open, with sight centered on a constant spot a few feet directly in front of one on a wall. One looks directly ahead rather than, say, down to the floor, because such encourages a more erect posture, which in turn fosters alertness and mitigates stiffness and back pain.

While *zazen* can be practiced by anyone at any time, it is often considered a social activity. While this can be as simple as a meeting of a group of friends or local Buddhist enthusiasts, it classically takes the form of the *sesshin*. A *sesshin* is a period of prolonged *zazen*, usually under the supervision of a *roshi* or leader of some sort. It is interrupted only by basic daily chores, meals, short sleep periods, and (frequently) dialogues with teachers. The *sesshin* is traditional of Japanese monastic practice (see Appendix I below), but in the West, it normally involves individuals who are not full-time monastic devotees. In this way, the *sesshin* is much like a conventional religious retreat, in that one temporarily withdraws from ordinary responsibilities in favor of quietism and contemplation. The purpose of such retreats, Zen or otherwise, is to make the contemplative life available to those who are unable (or unwilling) to pursue such as a full-time way of life.

The principal psychological product of the *sesshin* is boredom. Indeed, if there could ever be a "point" or purpose to the *sesshin*, it would be to induce boredom. Long periods of sitting, without movement or speech, precipitates stultifying boredom. This propensity is aggravated by the tendency to make the environment in which meditation takes place as mundane and uninteresting as possible. For this reason, the surface at which one stares is ordinarily a plain white wall, devoid of features or colors. Similarly, music or other overtly pleasing aural stimuli are absent.

The rationale for boredom and the environment that breeds it is clear: boredom frustrates the ego. The ego would prefer to meditate by a seashore, to have music playing, and to have the temperature regulated. The ego would prefer to move occasionally, to lie down, to get up from the floor now and then. Of course, the very reason the ego wants to avoid being bored is that it does not enjoy meditation, and this is the very reason for *zazen*. In other words, the ego-self wants to be entertained, it wants to experience particular things as part of its endless desire to be the experiencer of experience. By refusing to placate the ego, we are in effect forcing ourselves to cease this activity.

The *sesshin* thus helps to bring about awareness, or "awakeness," by frustrating the ego. The *sesshin* facilitates the dissolution of the ego by concentrating an enormous amount of frustration into a small period of time. The practice of zazen is greater than the sum of its parts, so that many hours of sitting for several consecutive days may help develop the necessary critical mass of frustration more quickly than would be possible outside of the *sesshin*.

III

Many people find the simplicity of *zazen* alienating. Just as Zen is confusing precisely because it so simple, *zazen* may appear intimidating precisely because it (seemingly) requires so little of the practitioner. While the physical dimension of *zazen* is structured, the actual mental point of the exercise is almost entirely undefined. The advice to "just sit" provides little in the way of concrete guidance. For this reason, it may be useful to discuss a variety of more specific meditational strategies that may be practiced either in conjunction with zazen or as a prelude to it (for a more personal account of meditational tactics, see Appendix II below).

One widely practiced beginning technique is the counting of breaths.[2] The purpose of this activity is to train the mind to focus on a non-personal, repetitive task. In focusing on counting you effectively distract the self so that the continual, unharnessed outpourings of the divided mind cease. Such counting is substantially more difficult than one imagines, in that boredom quickly sets in, followed by more interesting thoughts and ideas. A typical novice will be unable to reach ten before finding that he has lost track, with his mind somehow drifting off to other matters. When this happens, just begin again.

Similarly, when stray thoughts impose themselves into your counting, observe them but do not become involved with them. Watch them until they go away of their own accord and then resume counting. This process is much like daydreaming, so that you forget to concentrate upon the counting. Eventually, even the daydream becomes boring, and you remember that you are supposed to be counting. When this finally occurs, simply return to counting. In this way you extinguish intruding thoughts not by driving them out of consciousness but simply by turning concentration back to counting.

The mechanics are straightforward. A count is normally a complete inhalation and exhalation; if you prefer, you may count successively on each inhalation and exhalation. Some people find the latter less comfortable because of the natural pause people make after each full breath, in that it becomes a one-beat rather than a two-beat count. This can be distracting, but it also tends to focus concentration more tightly. Try both and settle on the cycle that is most comfortable and least distracting for you.

Although you can literally count each breath, many find it easier to count to ten and then repeat the one-to-ten cycle, throughout the duration of the exercise. By keeping the numbers small, one keeps the complexity of the task to a minimum, which makes it less difficult to get lost. As your experience grows, the pull of thoughts will lessen and the naturalness of counting breaths will become primary. Losing track will happen with less regularity as the act of counting becomes virtually automatic.

As an aid in this process, Paul Wienpahl suggests that when you exhale, you pretend the numbers are being drawn into your stomach.[3] After counting one, imagine that the number is there inside you. After reaching two, pretend that two is there beside it. As you fill yourself with numbers you are also drawing your "thoughts" inside yourself, making them, in effect, disappear. Eventually, you will find that other thoughts, and your mind itself, will similarly descend into the oblivion of your insides.

This process is basically one of exposing the true nature of the mind by forcing the individual to observe his or her own mental gymnastics. Through such observation, one sees thoughts come and go of themselves, without the aid of the conscious self. Thoughts appear and disappear of themselves, while the mind is busy counting breaths. In this way, the exercise illustrates the ego's continual demands for attention, while simultaneously demonstrating that such attention is not required. By learning to view the ego from a

127

dispassionate distance, one realizes that liberation from it is possible.

Counting breaths is a thoroughly non-personal form of meditation that depends upon distracting the mind from its own stream of consciousness. Another approach is to embrace this stream by specifically focusing on one's internal, self-generated thought processes. One of the best, and easiest, of such methods is the so-called "bubble meditation."[4] In this exercise, one approaches thoughts as if they were leaves floating upon the surface of a stream. One thinks of each "leaf" as if it were a "bubble" forming out of one's head, like the thoughts of a cartoon character. One observes each bubble for a short period of time—say 10 seconds or about the period of two breaths. When the time is up, move on to the next thought in the queue. If the same thought continues, or if nothing takes its place, simply let things be. Work with whatever the mind provides.

These thoughts should not be analyzed or pursued but merely observed as if they were someone else's. To use the cartoon analogy, imagine that a series of cartoons were passing before your eyes. You read the bubbles and then let them go, turning your attention to the next bubble that comes along. In terms of the leaf metaphor, it is as if you kept your gaze fixed on a single point and observed whatever drifted into (and out of) your line of sight.

The bubble works by labelling the mental programs as they run. Thinking about, say, tomorrow becomes filed away under that label. In this way, it is possible to take a dispassionate attitude toward thoughts, in that they are no longer identified as the self, but just as other objects of consciousness. In the same way that one learns to label material objects, it is possible to label thoughts automatically. In so doing, one objectifies one's own thoughts, so that they are external to oneself. It is as if one were doing nothing more than sorting the messages delivered into consciousness so that these messages are the only things one is aware of, rather than being a part of the person who is aware.[5]

In a strict sense, this bubble meditation is rather un-Zen-like, in that it involves the contemplation of the very thought processes we are trying to eliminate. However, this is, in fact, the rationale for the exercise, in that the first step in dissociating ourselves from the image of a person who "has" thoughts is the recognition that there is no one aside from experience. While the bubble is no substitute for *zazen*, the fact that it illustrates the arbitrariness of the thinker-thought distinction makes it a useful practice.

A third kind of meditation relies upon the repetitive chanting of some word or phrase. In many systems, such as the Tantra, Yoga, Transcendental Meditation (TM), and some schools of Christian mysticism, the repeated word (or mantra) is thought to have some kind of significance which is eventually experienced. It is sometimes suggested that repetition of a phrase (say, "Christ has risen") causes one to experience its veracity. In the Sufi tradition, one might chant "*Allah hu*," while in TM or various Indian sects, mantras are common Sanskrit words, letters, names of gods, or other Hindu benefactors. In any case, one's goal is essentially "one-pointedness," meaning that awareness is concentrated on a single point. As one becomes more successful in doing so, subtler levels of the "meaning" of the mantra meaning become apparent.[6]

In Zen, monks are often instructed to chant one of the sutras (while in the lotus position) before the formal commencement of *zazen*. One of the most popular is the so-called "Ten-Clause Sutra," which pays homage to the Bodhisattva (or Bosatsu) Kwanzeon:[7]

[Adoration to] Kwanzeon
Adoration to the Buddha!
To the Buddha we are related
In terms of cause and effect.

Depending upon the Buddha, the Dharma,
   and the Sangha,
[*Nirvana* is possible which is] eternal,
   ever-blessed, and free from defilements.
Every morning our thoughts are on Kwanzeon
Every evening our thoughts are on Kwanzeon
Every thought issues from the Mind,
Every thought is not separated from the Mind.

In general, such a practice is done more for the sake of ritual than for meditation, though the two are difficult to disentangle. Similarly, devotees of the (non-Zen) Pure Land school of Buddhism often chant the words "*namo-amitabhaya.*" In so doing, they are invoking the name of the buddha Amitabha, who is thought to live in a "pure land" to which others may migrate. Amitabha is revered because he pledged never to become a buddha until salvation was possible for all. Because he is indeed a buddha, such deliverance must be possible (as all Buddhist theory suggests). Invoking his name in a near-mantra-like fashion is thus a technique for avoiding attempts to become a buddha, in that it suggests that one has faith that he or she is already a buddha.

Such cultural artifacts aside, the utility of chanting is simply in focusing the mind away from itself. Just as we can count breaths to distract ourselves, we can also rhythmically chant for the same end. The phrase to be recited is itself unimportant and need have no meaning, special or otherwise. You may chant the name of a friend, a brand of breakfast cereal, or a nonsense word invented by your two-year-old. All that matters is that you occupy the mind with some mechanical activity so that the "true" mind can emerge in the space vacated by the ego.[8] In a more immediate sense, chanting ensures that the mind is concentrated on a single activity, that awareness is consigned entirely to this one activity. This is a Zen-like state, in that in the absence of self-consciousness, there is only chanting, rather than one who is chanting or one thinking about chanting.

IV

The awareness experienced while sitting can also be found in many other ordinary activities. Ultimately, we are introducing our lives to meditation, not meditation into our lives. Therefore, the spirit of meditation can be found in any activity, such as walking.

The choice of walking as an activity in which to find the spirit of meditation is appropriate because of the rhythmic, easy movement involved. Some experimentation on the use of different pace speeds can be used to give this sort of meditation a degree of variability. The activity also moves your total body through your environment; in so doing, you are exposed to a wider range of stimuli than encountered during sitting meditation.

It is helpful to begin using walking meditation as a part of regular daily sitting meditation. Sit, counting breaths, for approximately fifteen minutes. Then walk, as described below, for approximately five minutes, and then return to sitting for an additional five to ten minutes. It may be easier, given the circumstances of your meditative setting, to walk over a set distance, measuring by area rather than by time. For example, if the room in which you are meditating is large and spacious without many obstructions to a good-sized circuit of it, try walking around it four or five times. If the room is small or dangerously cluttered, try one or two circuits around your house or apartment building. If, however, you are required to circle a narrow, short track within one room, use a roughly constant time period.

Walking meditation, simply enough, meditates on walking. You should thus arise from sitting and compose your posture for a few seconds before you begin. Stand straight with your eyes focused on the floor ahead of you. Depending on your height, keep your head and chin comfortably erect; your eyes should be focused six to eight feet in front of you. Your arms hang relaxed at your sides with hands clasped in front, one hand held in a fist by the other, which cups it underneath. The hands should be held at a comfortable level permitting the elbows to be slightly bent or curved out toward the outward side. There should be no tension within the body.

Walk by taking short half-steps, i.e., lift one foot and place it down closely to the other with the heel meeting close to the instep of the stationary foot. The walk is heel-to-toe with each step being about one-half of a foot length, and the feet kept fairly close to each other. Men, with their naturally higher center of balance, may find that they easily lose their balance and sway to one side when doing this. To correct, widen the stance.

When counting breaths, one concentrates on counting; when walking, one concentrates on walking. Experience the movements of your body. Experiment with the pace of your steps. Feel the air as it moves around you. Listen to the floor squeak as you move. Smell the different odors in your path. Notice the difference between bare and shod feet. Feel your limbs move, your muscles flex and contract, your weight shift from foot to foot. In essence, through this meditation, "become" walking.

After your track has been covered, or the allotted time has expired, compose yourself at a stance. Then, sit and return to breath counting for the remainder of the exercise. This brings the whole practice to a close and helps keep a greater focus on the walking, because you are aware that you will return to sitting and not just stop and begin other tasks. In this way, you will not be tempted to consider something you had planned to do after your walking.

Many other physical activities can be used as a vehicle to experience meditative awareness. As with *zazen* or the counting of breaths, there is no goal. When one walks as described above, there is no greater purpose than to walk, to experience and "be" walking. In *zazen*, there is no other purpose than to sit. So it is with an array of activities that encompass some level of physical movement or skill. T'ai chi, karate, painting, dancing, flower arranging have all been traditionally employed as forms of meditation.

While it may be practical for some people to learn one of the activities which is commonly recognized as a historically useful meditative path, it may be much easier to choose an activity you already practice. Racquetball, jogging, or gardening are all equally amenable to meditative study. Even writing poetry or keeping a journal will do.[9]

Concentrate on a sport or hobby the next time you do it. Feel the small movements that comprise the activity. Sense the textures of the materials and the purpose of the tools that you use. Do not undertake a meditative approach with the idea or goal of improving your performance, in that to do so is to miss the point. Your "goal" is not to do "better," but simply to experience fully whatever it is you may be doing.

V

For many years European language commentaries on Zen placed little emphasis on *zazen*. This is perhaps most evident in the work of the late D.T. Suzuki, the most important and widely respected interpreter of Zen in the West. Though his *Essays in Zen Buddhism* was the standard English language work in the field for many years, it paid scant attention to meditation. Similarly, the first significant Westerner to write extensively about Zen, R.H. Blyth, also virtually ignores the subject. The first wave of indigenous literature in the West, best represented by the many books of Alan Watts, carried on the tradition of discussing Zen in terms of conventional philosophy.

While that tradition continues, particularly in the work of Masao Abe and others of the so-called Kyoto school, in the last twenty years there has been a sustained, and often quite virulent, attack upon the earlier approach by Western *roshis* trained in Japan (and their first-generation students). They have gone to considerable lengths to stress that *zazen* is not only necessary for the practice of Zen, but that Zen *is zazen*. As they see it, Suzuki's neglect of *zazen* resulted from the fact that meditation was so familiar and ingrained in his own culture that he took it for granted that it would be so in the West. It is also sometimes suggested that Suzuki purposely avoided *zazen* so as to interest Westerners who would otherwise have been alienated by this seemingly foreign practice. In either case, the new dogma rejects the intellectual approach in favor of Nipponese primitivism, arguing that work in the tradition of Suzuki or Watts is a trivial "popularization" that threatens the integrity of Zen.

In our view, the entire debate is misplaced in that it confuses *zazen* as method with *zazen* as end. Although it is axiomatic that meditation must be simultaneously method and end, the two are quite separate in terms of actual practice. In both Soto and Rinzai Zen it is apparent that, rhetoric aside, *zazen* is seen as the means to the end of enlightenment. Followers of these schools insist that the intellectual course is inherently flawed—inherently not Zen—because it suggests a different method, not because it suggests a different end.

As we have defined it, Zen is a state of waking consciousness in which dualistic thinking does not take place. Such a state is, again by definition, a meditative one. There is thus no dispute that Zen is effectively a state of meditation. The point of contention is one of how to achieve this state. The orthodox view is that it cannot be achieved by any way save that of *zazen*. Our position is that while *zazen* is a perfectly legitimate practice, it is only one of many ways toward Zen. In any event, the issue is ultimately irrelevant, in that, as an end, Zen is a contemplative state substantively identical to the experiential content of *zazen*.

The logic of presenting Zen in terms of concepts and theories is not because Zen can be reduced to these things, but because such an endeavor may help to foster the doubt necessary for the collapse of the edifice of the ego and the illusory world it maintains. In this way, philosophical argument plays the same role as *zazen*, the *sesshin*, and the *koan*. Still, these practices can only point the way. In the end, Zen is meditation.

APPENDIX I
The Monastic *Sesshin*

The word *sesshin* literally means "to collect thoughts."[10] Traditionally it is a period of intensive *zazen*, normally practiced once a month. These sessions consist of *zazen* from 3:00 or 3:30 a.m. till 10:00 p.m. for several consecutive days. The *sesshin* typically takes place in the *zendo* or meditation hall, where the students sleep as well. On each side of the hall is a raised platform or *tan* on which students both sleep and meditate. At the appointed hour, a bell is struck, the participants rise and store their bedding. After washing they repair to the lecture hall, where they (with a *roshi*) chant sutras for a short while. Following this they return to the *zendo* where they begin *zazen*.

An hour later they break for a simple breakfast, traditionally rice and pickles followed by tea. A bell sounds, a short break is observed, followed by two hours of *zazen* and a *sanzen* (student interview with a *roshi*). Students then break for either manual labor of some sort (another form of *zazen*), sutra chanting, a lecture on some point of Buddhism, or ritualized begging (which both supports the temple and teaches humility). An hour before noon, there is a meal, usually bean curd and more rice with pickles. There commences more chanting, followed by *zazen* (and, perhaps, *sanzen*).

In the late afternoon there is another interval for labor, followed by another meal of rice and pickles just before 5:00.

The remainder of the day (and evening) is devoted to *zazen*, punctuated only by *sanzen* and short (five minute) breaks for those who become too stiff or are otherwise unable to concentrate. At 10:00, a bell is again rung, tea is served, a sutra chanted, and then lights go out. At this point, many students go to the garden to sit for an hour. Most return to sleep (generally for no more than four hours), though some remain awake all night. At 3:00, the process resumes.

The *sesshin*, and the monastic life more generally, has a certain militaristic air about it. Life is highly regimented and structured, with strict rules regulating all behavior at virtually all times. Monks keep their heads shaved, for much the same reason that marine recruits do. An attendant walks the *zendo* caring the *keisaku* or warning stick, with which he strikes anyone who appears to be drowsing or otherwise lacking in concentration.

This sort of boot-camp approach infuses the life of the monk with rituals which—whatever their redeeming qualities—are quite foreign to much of the spirit of Zen. If Zen is a reaction to the artificialities of convention, it seems odd to mire training in a sea of rigid conventions. The old masters placed considerable emphasis on avoiding dogma. To illustrate their rejection of convention, they sometimes burned sutras and went so far as to suggest, "If you see the Buddha, kill the Buddha." The point, of course, was to deny the importance or relevance of any symbol or tradition, including those of the sutras and the Buddha himself.

Monastic practice as described above clings to tradition, almost to the point of mistaking it with the substance of Zen. The implicit attitude is that one does what one is told for no reason other than one is told to do it. One accepts the authority of the monastic order on the faith that the order knows what is best. Acolytes thus take a "master" in the literal sense of that term, implying that they place themselves completely in the spiritual care of a teacher or *roshi*.

Of course, there is nothing inherently wrong or misguided about this Nipponese tradition. It is quite likely that our hostility to accepting its insistence on blind faith is a cultural artifact of an individualistic social ideology. However, if that is the case, it is equally true that the authoritarian, monastic approach is equally an artifact of a collectivist culture. If so, then conventional forms of Japanese practice and training may be gleefully abandoned as inappropriate to the West.

A more recent incident—a *mondo* of sorts—suggests precisely this notion.[11] An American was visiting a Zen temple in Japan. He observed with disdain that the abbot escorting him stopped to bow to various statues of the *bodhisattva* as they walked. Finally, he expressed his agitation by saying that he thought a true follower of Zen was above all this nonsense and should be free to spit on such ridiculous icons. "Okay," replied the abbot in the best English he could manage, "you spits, I bows."

It is in this spirit that we propose that *roshis*, the *sesshin*, and to a lesser degree, even *zazen* itself, be viewed from the perspective of utility. There is surely nothing wrong with traditional methods, just as there is nothing amiss in bowing to the image of a *bodhisattva*. By the same token, there is no necessary reason to follow them, just as there is no necessity for bowing. The question is one of cultural and personal values.

In any event, Japanese methods are not Zen. They, like this book, are merely means to an end. Just as Zen cautions against confusing ideas with reality, sanity argues against installing one set of arbitrary cultural ideas as the only acceptable method of practicing Zen.

APPENDIX II
Personal Observations on Meditative Practice

Like any new activity that one attempts to cultivate, it can be difficult to make meditation a regular part of one's life. There is often hesitation or resistance, because one is not sure that one is "doing it right" or because the time spent could be more wisely devoted to tasks that are considered more critical or routine, like grocery shopping, paying bills, or even writing books.

One needs to find a small portion of the day in which to meditate regularly. To start, only small portions of time are required—from ten to twenty minutes every day or even every other day. It is recommended that one meditate in the morning, preferably before breakfast. The point is to be neither too hungry from the day's demands, nor too physically preoccupied (and hence sleepy) with the digestion of food. Above all, just meditate—whenever you can, however often you can.

One of the best ways to overcome one's own inertia is to socialize your meditative practice by becoming involved with a local Zen community. Such groups are typically highly informal, fluid in membership, and thoroughly receptive to beginners. Many college towns in the United States have a Zen group, as do most cities of any size.

Groups are valuable for several reasons. First, they provide hands-on instruction on how to meditate. Second, they provide an arena in which to discuss your experiences and problems. The group acts very much like a support group in which you meet like-minded people who are likely to be encountering the same difficulties and doubts as you. Third, the fact that there are other people sitting on the floor staring at the wall may make you feel less foolish for doing so. Fourth, by going to a group meeting you have effectively forced yourself to meditate for at least the duration of the meeting. You may find it much easier to walk or drive to the meeting than to force yourself to sit motionless for an hour. By binding yourself to the meeting, you have tied your own hands, requiring yourself to do something you might otherwise not have the energy or patience to do.

Remember, the purpose of meditation is simply to meditate. Awareness, awakening, is a process that evolves as mental programs slow and insight is found. Meditation, like the *Tao*, is goal-less. It provides a path to be experienced. Do not find yourself falling into the habit of sharing your experiences with others in the group in such a way as to foster a competitive atmosphere. One does not meditate any better than anyone else. Meditation is a process without end, without goals. You may never experience something someone else does, so do not chart your experiences in terms of progress toward something. Meditate and stay with the group, but keep yourself and others from becoming competitive. The group should produce and provide an atmosphere for developing freedom from the societal constraints to which we are all accustomed. Again, there is no "right" way to do it. You are not doing it "wrong," and a group situation should help, not hinder this recognition.

In formal Rinzai practice, the *koan* is often studied in tandem with *zazen*. Strictly speaking, a *koan* should be studied only under a *roshi*, in that much of the learning process derives from the *sanzen*, or interview between student and *roshi*. Given that it would be odd for the Rinzai establishment to suggest that the *roshi* is unnecessary, the advice about avoiding the *koan* in an untutored context should be viewed with some skepticism. On the other hand, it may well be that much of the value of the *koan* is lost in the hands of one who is not trained in its use. In any case, there is little to be lost—save patience—in pondering *koans* on your own.

Work with a *koan* may be particularly useful after some practice with breath counting. At this point there is often a growing feeling of resistance or uselessness with the practice of meditation. The student must realize that this resistance comes from the ego, and that this point in time should be viewed as an opportunity to go further. The *koan* may provide a vehicle for such progress.

While several collections of traditional Japanese *koans* are readily available, it may be profitable to devise your own.[12] Everyone faces a number of suitable *koan*-like questions in everyday life. The human quest for metaphysical understanding usually begins with the reflexive question "Who am I?" It is possible to personalize this question into a *koan* by using your own first name. Puzzle out for yourself who this person is, what his or her place is in the world, whether this person is unique. Find out what constitutes this person, what separates him or her from the rest of experience, and who it is that wants to know these things.

In much the same way, it is possible to devise other *koans* from clues given you by your environment.[13] Are there any specific problems that you are experiencing? Is there anyone you are particularly concerned about? Is there an event coming up in your life from which you seek greater significance? Form a *koan* that concerns this question by streamlining it to one or two words. Contemplate this phrase for ten to twenty minutes for several consecutive days. Insight will continue through this practice as the subject of the *koan* continues to have significance in your life. Unfamiliar solutions may develop through this practice as the mind begins to dissect and ponder the phrase in question.

Regardless of how one meditates, it is important to remember that the practice requires patience. Although *satori* cannot be approached in stages, meditation can. Like any other new and unusual activity, time is required to become acclimated. Similarly, the more and longer you meditate, the easier and more rewarding you will find it. It is much like learning to ride a bicycle: you may find it confusing and discouraging in the beginning, but if you keep with it, you discover that it is a perfectly natural activity.

NOTES

1. This, and subsequent quotes from Hui-neng, are from Wong Mou-Lam, *The Sutra of Wei Lang (Hui-neng)* (London: Luzac, 1944).
2. Beginners are often instructed to count as part of their *zazen* practice; they assume the lotus position and begin the breathing exercise. Later, work on a *koan* may be substituted for counting. Eventually, there is only *zazen* without any kind of "crutch."
3. Paul Wienpahl, *The Matter of Zen* (New York: New York University Press, 1964).
4. For a discussion, see Lawrence LeShan's aptly titled *How to Meditate* (New York: Bantam, 1977).
5. For a discussion of labelling as a method, see Charlotte Joko Beck, *Everyday Zen: Love and Work* (New York: Harper and Row, 1989).
6. Transcendental Meditation is by far the most well known meditative practice in the United States. It employs the mantra for the sake of transcending ordinary experience so as to achieve unity with the stream of cosmic consciousness. The achievement of this unity is thought to bring about profound benefits for the practitioner such that all desires and material cravings, feelings of low self-esteem or shame are transcended, yielding a state of blissful awakening. In this way, TM is a skill or technique for "self-actualization," in much the way that jogging or aerobics are a means to the end of fitness. To study TM is thus to pursue a method of self-improvement, as if charting a passage over a spiritual sea.
7. D.T. Suzuki, *Manual of Zen Buddhism* (New York: Grove Press, 1960), p. 16. See also Wienpahl, *The Matter of Zen*, chapter 14.

8. Compare this approach with that of Christian mysticism. To take the prototypical example of the Hesychasm, one meditates so as to "purify" the self so as to achieve union with God. The method for such purification is devotion to Jesus Christ through the recitation of the so-called Jesus Prayer. One continuously repeats the prayer, mantralike, calling upon Jesus to help attain a pure heart by repeatedly pleading, "Lord Jesus Christ, Son of God, have mercy on me!" One thus chants to cleanse the soul, so as to make possible (re-)union with God.

9. For a spirited discussion, see Natalie Goldberg, *Writing Down the Bones* (Boston: Shambhala, 1986).

10. Among the many excellent discussions of the *sesshin* and monastic life in general are D.T. Suzuki's now somewhat dated *Training of the Zen Buddhist Monk* (Kyoto, Japan: Eastern Buddhist Society, 1934); his *Introduction to Zen Buddhism* (New York: Grove Press, 1964); and Wienpahl, *The Matter of Zen*. The following discussion draws heavily from these sources.

11. Reported in Weinpahl, *The Matter of Zen*, p. 43-4.

12. Two standard collections, available in many editions and with different commentaries, are the *Mumonkan* and the *Hekiganroku*.

13. See James Whitehill, *Enter the Quiet* (New York: Harper and Row, 1980).

CHAPTER SEVEN

Beyond Convention:
The Social Implications of Zen

The conflict between right and wrong is a disease of the mind.

—Seng-ts'an

The philosophers have heretofore interpreted the world; the thing, however, is to change it.

—Karl Marx

Our concern to this point has been with Zen as an individual level phenomenon—that is, we have examined the consequences of Zen for the structure of the human psyche. As is apparent, though, patterns of individual thought both mold and are molded by the social order. Hence, what may appear to be strictly a matter of personal philosophy can have important social implications. For that reason, this final chapter addresses the "social theory" implicit in Zen—that is, the implications of Zen for culture, politics, and society.

II

The closest Western approximation to the social philosophy inherent in both Zen and Taoism is found in the work of the utopian socialists and anarchists of the nineteenth century. While in conversational English the word anarchy is used as a pejorative synonym for chaos, it has a much different meaning in political philosophy, where it denotes not so much opposition to order but only to order predicated upon coercion. As Lao-tzu observed, the ability of some individuals to control the lives of others is "unnatural," in the sense that it is contrary to human nature. In this way, the anarchist denounces not only the state, but all social arrangements that institutionalize or otherwise support the ability to coerce others. This coercion takes a myriad of forms, such as the drafting of young men to serve in armies, the subjugation of women, and the exploitation of workers by the owners of capital.

Coercion, it is argued, is inherently corruptive, in that it displaces natural benevolence. Power corrupts not only those who wield it, but those who are its victims. To take a whimsical (but illustrative) example, consider Ebenezer Scrooge. As a wealthy moneylender, Scrooge has become psychologically warped in the process of becoming prosperous. As the anarchist might suggest, much of that warpage results from his ability to treat other people as the means to the end of making profits. By holding the threat of financial ruin or debtor's prison over people's heads, it is not only the victims that become psychologically impaired, but also Scrooge himself. The good-natured and caring young man is replaced by the scheming and hateful old man, with the metamorphosis accomplished through the counting of gold.

In the so-called state of nature before the advent of coercion—or Scrooge before his alteration—life is characterized by the Taoist principle of *wu-wei*. Leaving nature to run its course without unnecessary intervention, humans live in a condition of spontaneous cooperation. They co-exist peacefully, ordering and coordinating their affairs naturally, without the aid of policemen or tax collectors. As Marx would later suggest, goods and services are produced with individuals contributing according to ability and receiving according to need. The entire system is self-regulating, functioning quite nicely without authority structures. This anarchy is not chaotic; it is naturally harmonious. It is not a world devoid of order, but one in which order comes about by itself, in much the same way that the sun rises and sets.

From this perspective, the social pathologies characterizing modern society are not a function of the shortcomings of the human personality but of the artificial power relationships that have disrupted the natural equilibrium that would otherwise obtain. Unconsciously and unknowingly, we have intervened in nature, contra *wu-wei*, so as to make possible the conditions under which the wealthy control the lives of the poor, owners control workers, men rule women, and whites colonize and enslave people of color. In so doing, we have perverted the "proper" or natural mode of human civilization, producing instead an ersatz world of violence, greed, and war.

Hobbes described the resulting situation as a perpetual war of everyone against everyone, in which life is "poor, brutish, nasty, and short." For Hobbes and the entire Judeo-Christian tradition, this "law of the jungle" is assumed to be inherent in the human character. We are naturally aggressive, amoral, and animalistic, so that in the absence of sharply defined social controls we will be trapped in an endless war of all against all. For the anarchists, such a view inverts cause and effect. The logic of the jungle is not natural to men but results precisely from the attempt to create a rigid social order. Social conventions regulating thought and behavior are thus not an answer but the problem itself.

Implicit in this argument is the realization that there are no absolutes, in that it is only in the absence of absolute values that genuine liberty is possible. This is entirely obvious when we consider that if liberty means anything, it means a society that is tolerant of differences in opinion and values. Such tolerance is possible only when we reject claims to absolute knowledge, because the belief in such knowledge provides the vehicle through which we impose our sense of Truth on others. The Catholic church, for example, claims absolute knowledge in regard to reproductive rights, so that it attempts to prohibit abortion, birth control, artificial insemination, and so on. In the same way, many people attempt to pass judgement about what sort of books other people may read, because they believe they know, absolutely, what should and should not be read. The failed experiments of the "people's democracies" of Eastern Europe did not feel obligated to trust the people to rule, because they divined the Truth from Leninist theory. Similarly, the "Islamic republics" of Iran and Saudi Arabia deduce their principles from the Koran, so that it is entirely meaningless to suggest popular control of public policy, since, if Truth is known, the transient desires of the masses are irrelevant. In sum, liberty requires not only that no one has the ability to impose their values on others, but that no one has the desire to do so.

For that reason, the anarchist rejects all claims of absolutes, in that such are contrary to the spirit of true freedom. To the Judeo-Christian mind, this is the epitome of madness. The cause of such alarm, of course, is grounded in a theory of human nature which sees behavior driven by the egoistic pursuit of the objects of desire. Morality is thus the process by which people overcome their baser instincts. The Eastern tradition, however, takes the rather different position that our nature is not something to struggle against or overcome. Left to their own devices, free of Commandments, Freud's superego, or social conventions of any kind, people will not become beasts. The problem is not in the "immorality" of anarchy but in the thoroughly odd view of human nature that makes notions of morality appear necessary.

This point is made most strongly by the giant of modern anarchism, Pierre-Joseph Proudhon (1809–65).[1] Proudhon argued that rapacity and malevolence—in effect, all human evil—derive from the artificial structure of social and political hierarchies. Human beings find themselves trapped in a strange and hostile environment, much like animals imprisoned in a zoo. Just as such animals are often violent and confused—just as they often do not seem to behave and think as they do in their natural habitat—human beings tend to be alienated and confused, so that they often react irrationally and violently. For both man and animal, the solution is freedom, not better cages.

This is also the point of Rousseau's oft-quoted dictum that "men are born free yet they are everywhere in chains."[2] We are naturally free but are bound by the chains of repressive and unnatural social relations. Remove the chains, allow men and women to be free again, and we will have taken significant steps toward solving our most pressing problems. In other words, remove inhibiting and constricting power structures and the accompanying social ills will disappear. To free ourselves as a society, we must first free ourselves as individuals. In this way, liberty becomes not only an end in itself, but the means to the greater end of human happiness. Anarchy is thus a decidedly *social* doctrine, its moral force deriving not only from its demands for individual freedom, but from its emphasis on freedom for others and the human species in toto.

Of course, Rousseau's chains are not merely the coercion that comes at the barrel of a gun but any socially defined attempt to limit freedom of conscience. As we have seen, and as Rousseau implicitly suggests, freedom is limited by the entire edifice of social convention. Social customs of all kind stand in the way of liberty by virtue of the fact that they not only circumscribe certain behaviors, but they artificially demarcate the world into arbitrary categories and classes. Languages, religions, states, and societies themselves become nothing more than nested sets of prisons.

The anarchist sees social institutions as standing in the way of personal liberty, which in turn impedes the development of a natural, cooperative social order. Zen takes this logic one step forward by suggesting that it is not merely power relationships that are at fault, but the entire notion of a socially-defined reality. Both the anarchist and the Buddhist see human beings as enslaved to arbitrary social conventions that have been mistaken for real things. The former denounces the artificiality of social status, while the latter opposes the illusion of the socially-defined ego. For the anarchist, we are trapped within a false and pernicious world where social relationships have become so entrenched as to produce social evils; for the Buddhist, we are confined in a world of collectively sanctioned abstractions that have become so rigid as to alienate ourselves from our own lives.

151

Anarchist theory calls for the destruction of the present social order so that a more genuine and humane one may evolve, just as Zen suggests that one see through convention to the true reality that emerges in its wake.

Zen is thus a kind of conceptual anarchy, maintaining that the chains that bind and degrade human nature are not merely in our relationships with one another but in the very way that we have chosen to view the world. In our reliance upon conceptual maps of experience, we institute the psychological equivalent of society, in that these maps come to stand in the way of our true nature. Just as an artificial society debases our lives by instituting unnatural social relationships, the synthetic world of conceptual abstractions alienates the self from experience by manufacturing a false division between experience and the person who has experience. In both cases, the solution is to eliminate the corrupting influence, so as to return to a "natural" society devoid of coercive relationships and a "natural" or unified self in which there is no one aside from experience.

III

Proudhon's immediate targets were the social practices that enthroned certain people as de facto masters of others. This, in turn, implied an indictment of institutions, such as capitalism and private property, that unfairly produced inequalities in power or status. More fundamentally, though, the real issue was not these practices per se, but the set of ideas and values which supported and sustained them. In this way, Proudhon was ultimately concerned with the intellectual foundations of the established order. The program for social change associated with his name is thus predicated upon a criticism of prevailing social norms, in that to sweep away the old order we must first discredit the ideas which perpetuate it.

This campaign does not deny the possibility or morality of any social values. Instead, it merely suggests that current values result from, and are maintained by, political and economic inequalities. Anticipating arguments later made by Marx, Proudhon implied that the ruling ideas of any society are the ideas of the ruling class. In other words, the economically dominant class creates and maintains a set of values and orientations which, while parading under the putative endorsement of God or human nature, are in fact designed to defend the privileges and interests of the ruling class. The ideas of property rights and so-called free enterprise, for example, become social norms because they protect the capitalist class from appropriation of "its" property by the working class. Similarly, freedom becomes defined in negative terms, meaning that it is to be found in the absence of constraints that limit one's liberty rather than in the existence of provisions that positively contribute to liberty by making it possible. In the same way, the economically powerful establish what amounts to a caste system, with different occupations and levels of monetary achievement associated with different levels of status in the social hierarchy.

To the ruling class and their bourgeois allies, these values are somehow implicit in the natural order. Private property is a "natural right," so that any attempt to redistribute wealth or institute collective ownership of the means of production is seen, as James Madison put it, as "wicked and improper." By the same logic, the "right" of individuals and corporations to dominate the working class through their control over access to livelihoods becomes seen as equally "natural," as does the entire system of economic production and the social relations that are derived from it. More generally, the coercive potential of the dominant class defines the sphere of social rewards and sanctions. It is "theft," for example, to take other people's property, but not theft to appropriate labor through the institution of "profits." In this fashion, the unequal distribution of power that results from capitalist economics is generalized through all aspects of society, eventually coming to dominate the entire social order.

It is through this process that Rousseau's chains are formed. Born free, human beings find themselves immediately confined within an ersatz world of convention, in which these conventions are largely determined by an insular ruling class. From the vantage point of Zen, the issue is deeper still: the prison of convention is not limited to the maligning influence of social coercion, but to the entire process of (largely socially-defined) conceptual abstraction. It is not merely that social norms are an artifact of unequal power relationships, but the fact that these norms exist—or rather, that they are mistaken for things that have some kind of inherent validity. If the anarchist dismisses contemporary society as the unjust child of a perverse distribution of economic resources, the Taoist and Buddhist see farther by denouncing the entire process by which we confuse abstractions with concrete reality.

Proudhon and Marx view social norms as arbitrary and capricious, because they enforce the ideas of one class over those of others. However insightful, this proposition is ultimately incomplete, in that all ideas are arbitrary, including those of Proudhon and Marx. In other words, it is not the content of social ideas—whether they are more or less fair or more or less just—but the fact that there are *any* social ideas. All such systems constitute what amounts to a collective definition of reality. Yet, as we have seen, reality cannot be fit into the dualistic categories implied by the notion of definition. The principal effect of our society is thus not only the injustice of an arbitrary scheme of social rewards and punishments based upon economic attainment, but in the creation of ideas and values which are, by definition, empty.

Accordingly, Rousseau's prison of convention cannot be destroyed by (only) declaring a war upon the ideas of the ruling class, but only by declaring a war upon all ideas. In this sense, Zen is a call to a revolution, but one radically different than that envisioned by Marxists. Rather than rebellion against (only) exploitation and injustice, Zen suggests rebellion against the social theories that make exploitation and injustice possible. In this way, Zen rejects all concepts, including those of society, anarchy, capitalism, Marxism, exploitation, injustice, and revolution. This revolt is not (only) against our political and economic masters, but against the tyranny of convention.[3]

In renouncing concepts, Zen is thus an insurrection against the entire structure of reality as we know it. Zen is thus opposed to *everything*, including the idea of Zen itself.

IV

The opposition to ideas is not equivalent to opposition to the "substance" of these ideas. To reject the idea of justice, say, is not to deny that individuals are in some sense responsible for their actions. It is instead to refuse to accept an abstract, rarefied theory of justice as an end in itself. In the same way, to discard the idea of goodness is not to endorse evil, but merely to recognize that both good and evil are empty, formless ideas that arise mutually. Like all dualistic opposites, good and evil are not aspects of experience, but judgmental labels attached to experience by the ego. Like black and white, or left and right, they exist only in subjective relationship to one another, so that by subscribing to the notion of good, one necessarily brings evil into existence. Hence, in casting aside good, one becomes free of evil.

If there is such a thing as Original Sin or the fall of man, it consists precisely in coming to believe in good without evil. The forbidden fruit was thus not "knowledge," but "illusion," in that it consisted of nothing more than the advent of dualism. Armed with these new ideas, human beings went on to spin enormously elaborate religious-ethical systems based upon the strict observance of rules of conduct. Even in the secular tradition of Western academic philosophy, the study of ethics has been devoted to discovering general rules by which to regulate human behavior. Christians believe that such rules are to be found in the Bible. The Utilitarians thought they could deduce such rules from self-evident principles, such as the greatest good for the greatest number. Even Kant believed he could deduce from experience the so-called categorical imperative (or "golden rule") to treat other persons as ends rather than means.

This emphasis upon stringent rules also dominates everyday ethical decisions: most people decide what to do by consulting abstract principles that they think should guide a "good" person. In much the same vein, Freud went so far as to consider it a psychological disorder to be unable or unwilling to engage in abstract moral reasoning, i.e., he implies that one should be able to specify the proper thing to do by being told a set of factual conditions. To the Western mind, then, immorality is the absence of rules, so that their renunciation is tantamount to nihilism.

The need to defend civilization against such nihilism is uniformly defended in terms of the need to keep animalistic desires in check. Tainted with the curse of Cain, and otherwise inherently prone to "sin," humans require a conscience versed in God's canon. In this view, to be human is much like being one of the beasts surgically turned into men by H.G. Wells's allegorical Doctor Moreau. Driven by the desires and wants of animals, yet forced to walk upright and wear clothes, these creatures are constantly torn between their natural savagery and the rules assigned them by Moreau. Their lives are thus a constant struggle—the animal battles with the man, the spirit with the flesh. These psuedo-men are thus forever in fear of Moreau's wrath if they break the rules he has established.

Western civilization, even in these supposedly enlightened and secular times, tacitly endorses this view of human nature. Rather than original sin, it may be argued that it is self-interest and the desire for power that drives our antisocial tendencies. In any case, civilized beings must follow rules to prevent their natural proclivity for aggression and misanthropy. Thus to suggest that we abandon all axiomatic ethical systems as arbitrary nonsense is the epitome of madness. Without rules, it is said, without a sense of justice to overcome our immoral pursuit of self-interest, society will devolve into a libertine orgy of chaos and destruction. People will become barbarous monsters, oblivious to the needs or suffering of others. Without the constraints of social rules, life will be reduced once more to Hobbes's war of all against all.

From the perspective of Proudhon or Lao-tzu, this argument is transparently mistaken in that it is based upon a false assumption about the natural condition of the human species. The fact that human beings appear so desperately in need of rules to check their avarice is because they are no longer in a natural state. In other words, in the state of nature, human beings do not have any rules precisely because they don't need rules. Left to nature, humans are peaceful and cooperative, living together in a kind of spontaneous order. It is only when subjected to the manufactured rules of society—only when removed from their natural condition—that social pathologies manifest themselves. In this way, the social (as opposed to natural) order is a deviation from *wu-wei*, suggesting a deviation from the *Tao*. Of course, to cling to ethical rules is only to stray further from the *Tao* by introducing more contrivances.

What the theologian and the philosopher see as the solution is, in fact, the very problem itself. Human nature has indeed "fallen," but only by abandoning *wu-wei*. To

157

affect a cure, it is thus necessary to return to nature, not to flee from it. Put differently, the problem of evil is a direct result of clinging to good, so that the solution is to dispose of both.

Seen thus, good and evil are different manifestations of the same dualistic process. It is thus not necessary to deny that there are things that one might reasonably label as good or bad, but only that to buy into this process of labelling, we have to have both bad and good simultaneously. Like any other dualistic pattern, the two sides result from the same mental process. As Lao-tzu puts it,

> When everyone recognizes beauty as beautiful,
>   there is already ugliness
> When everyone recognizes goodness as good,
>   there is already evil.

Thus to pursue good alone—to try to eliminate all evil—is literally impossible, for the same reason that you cannot eliminate the South by moving North. As Alan Watts observes, "Good without evil is like up without down," so that "to make an ideal of pursuing good is like trying to get rid of the left by turning constantly to the right. One is therefore compelled to go round in circles."[4]

Ultimately, there is no left or right, just as there is no good or evil. There is only whatever there is, so that the process of labelling is not only redundant, but potentially dangerous if one confuses these labels with real things. Such notions are only more abstractions, and, as such, more conceptual baggage to overcome. Because Zen implicitly denies the reality of justice or morality, it is sometimes criticized as being immoral and providing a justification for self-obsession. By denying the validity of simple notions of right and wrong, it is said, Zen shows itself to be a vacuous, nihilistic rationalization for selfishness and complacency.

While Zen certainly does suggest that morality is something to be transcended, it does not imply the kind of

Nietzschean superman that its critics would have us believe. One liberated from socially-defined moral conventions is not one who has no regard for the happiness or security of his fellows. Instead, the liberated person sees such conventions for what they are: artificial, socially-defined rules lacking any necessarily compelling moral force. To be sure, some of these rules—say, prohibitions against murder—make good sense, but others—say, state sanctioned heterosexual monogamy in the form of marriage—are entirely arbitrary. Further, many social conventions (as we have seen) are established in the interests of the groups capable of enforcing them. Thus, it is "murder" to kill a human being for the sake of stealing a wallet, but it is only a regrettable accident when a person dies in a work-related industrial accident. The fact that more people die every day on the job through such accidents than are "murdered," is irrelevant: strict enforcement of occupational safety programs would reduce profitability, so that industry is socially-sanctioned to allow preventable deaths in the name of free enterprise.

V

The danger of taking seriously such arbitrary notions as good and evil is readily demonstrated by the fact that most of the world's suffering results not from the conscious pursuit of evil but from the pursuit of good. Indeed, even a cursory survey of Western history suggests that the greatest human evils are invariably perpetuated in the name of good. The Inquisition, colonialism, the "white man's burden," the atomic infernos of Hiroshima and Nagasaki, the Cultural Revolution, apartheid, and even the killing fields of Cambodia resulted not from purposeful evil, but from crusades for moral and political justice. The entire Second World War was predicated upon mindless abstractions of racial superiority and *Lebensraum*. Even Nazi genocide was based upon a theory of eugenics and racial superiority, supposedly for

159

the greater glory of the human race. While surely the darkest episode in modern history, it resulted from a Manichean view of the world in which the righteous must combat evil. As Bob Dylan observes, "Though they murdered six million . . . The Germans too had God on their side."

It is the twisted view of one's self, or one's cause, as being "good," of being derived from higher principles of politics or religion, that causes a seemingly endless plethora of social ills. The pursuit of good as a real entity, as opposed to a conventionally-defined abstraction like liters or miles, encourages people to take these ideals over their own innate nature. In the process, they abandon their humanity in favor of morality or righteousness, which in turn allows them to engage in acts of violence and intolerance. Witches were burned alive for their own good, to save their souls. Crusaders killed and maimed Arabs to secure the "holy land"—a practice that is carried on today by the Israeli army. In every American city, there are groups actively campaigning to limit the rights of other people in the name of God or Truth. Every day, women are harassed as they enter abortion clinics because some people want to prevent others from controlling their own bodies; books are removed from school libraries because some people want to dictate what others will read; drugs are made illegal because some people want to determine what others will put in their bodies; homosexuals are discriminated against because some people want to control the sort of sexual behavior that other people engage in; and so on. In each of these examples, repression is rationalized by the belief of some individuals that their values and opinions are Right, while those of others are Wrong.

This perplexing tendency to take abstractions as real manifests itself in what is euphemistically referred to as "national security policy." Since the advent of the Cold War, our leaders have been willing and happy to wage wars against civilian populations in places like Vietnam, Guatemala, El Salvador, and Nicaragua for no reason aside from an unfathomable set of infantile geopolitical abstractions. In the same way, they repeatedly were willing to risk thermonuclear war over the issue of whether we should have a planned economy. Given the number of corpses produced by the Cold War conflict over ideas, it is difficult to argue with the proposition that the world would have been a much better place in the absence of these ideas—or, rather, in the absence of confusing them with things worth killing millions of people over.

From the perspective of Zen, all abstract notions of right and wrong lend themselves to perversion, in that to pursue one side of the dualistic relationship between polar opposites is to buy into a game that cannot be won. In our interpretation, Zen suggests that we abandon all such abstractions and leave the conduct of human affairs to the naturally benevolent disposition of humanity. Unhindered by the oppressive weight of doing good, the world becomes a better place. Put another way, much of the evil of the world could be done away with if we simply stopped thinking in terms of good and evil, i.e., if we let people be whatever it is they are. Conventions introduce dangerous forms of insanity that cause people to sacrifice their humanity, as manifested in such oxymorons as "Christian soldiers" or "war for the sake of peace."

Although Zen denies the reality of good and evil, it does not reduce to the platitude that "whatever is, is right." A Zen master mourns at the death of a friend. He or she may weep at a tour of Treblinka and feel anger or grief over poverty or racism. To accept reality as it is, without the benefit of pre-programmed concepts, is not to say that one has to enjoy or be resigned to that reality. For the same reason that Zen suggests that "When hungry, eat; when tired, sleep," it does not deny that some things may be undesirable or that they should be changed. Instead, Zen suggests that the realization of those facts come naturally and spontaneously, not from a conscious desire to do what is right. Just as sleeping when not tired may cause torpor, and eating when not hungry obesity, doing right rather than doing what is natural may also have deleterious consequences. To deny right and wrong or pleasure and pain is not to suggest that one should not care for others or that one should not remove a burning hand from the flames. Rather, it is to maintain that all efforts to do anything should flow from precisely the same kind of incentive that comes from removing your hand from an open flame. When being burned, you move your hand spontaneously and naturally, without first deciding what your abstract notions of pleasure and pain suggest that you do. Similarly, rather than stopping to help a pedestrian hit by a passing auto because you reason that it is the morally correct thing to do, Zen suggests you do it because it is natural for you to do so.

Zen thus suggests that, much like charity, saving the world begins at home. To truly save the world, you first must save yourself—and the world—from your very attempts to do so. Action must come about naturally, spontaneously and unencumbered with conceptual explanation. Messianic self-righteousness, no matter how sincere and well-intentioned, is merely feeding your own imaginary ego and, in the process, creating more of the evil that you seek to destroy. If we wish to live in a world devoid of evil, we must first be free of good.

VI

The true basis of despotism lies in our way of perceiving the world and ourselves. Ultimately, the greatest source of oppression is not guns but ideas. Both individuals and the societies they comprise tend to be preoccupied with dualistic abstractions they confuse for real things. While political and economic repression are all too real, a final solution to these problems can be found only by ending the modes of thought which make such repression intellectually and culturally acceptable. Genuine social emancipation, then, must begin with individuals freeing themselves from the obfuscation inherent in social convention. This is the spirit in which we think of Zen as a method of liberation.

NOTES

1. Proudhon's major works are *What is Property* and *The General Idea of the Revolution in the Nineteenth Century*. Both are available in a variety of translations.
2. The phrase is from the first sentence of *The Social Contract*. The same sentiments are expressed in his *Discourse on the Origins of Inequality* and, to a lesser degree, in *Emile*.
3. Marx himself sometimes seemed to endorse something approximating this notion. As he saw it, the "individual" as normally understood was simply a facade behind which stood the social forces constituting society. The individual (as ego) is thus an "ensemble of social relations" rather than an autonomous personality. Emancipation, then, must finally encompass a state in which individuals are no longer socially determined.
4. Alan Watts, *The Way of Zen* (New York: Vintage, 1989), pp. 115-16.

EPILOGUE
Understanding Zen

Death solves all problems. No man, no problems.
   —Josef Stalin

No one understands Zen.
   —R.H. Blyth

More than simply a fitting epitaph to the barbarism of his life, Stalin's words provide a commendable summary of the human condition. As he suggests, death is the one genuine "solution" to the problems that haunt our lives. All methods of transcendence, including Zen, are ultimately useless if we hope to find in them a panacea by which the pain of being human can be magically eliminated. Zen is an answer only to the extent that we realize that the effort of seeking an answer is a part of the very pain we wish to escape. While Zen does provide an exit from the existential predicament, it does so by eliminating the barriers that separate people from experience, not by providing avenues by which to escape that experience.

Ultimately, pain is pain. Existential salvation is found in the acceptance of our lives; it offers no defense against the reality that life is not always pleasant. One does not need a rigid ego to find frostbite uncomfortable or to mourn at the death of a parent. Zen is not a physical or psychological anesthetic which numbs us to pain or sorrow, but a perspective from which these things are seen for what they (i.e., we) are.

To again paraphrase Masao Abe, to be alive is to be a problem to oneself.[1] The solution is not to be rid of problems (i.e., life), but to cease objecting to life. By clinging to Zen as if it were a talisman that could protect us from pain is to mistake the mental construct called "Zen" for something that exists. This, of course, is the same conceptual error that is the source of all our difficulties in making sense of the world. If "understanding Zen" means anything at all, it is understanding the limits of understanding, as it were, rather than in adding an abstract, intellectualized Zen to the myriad of other conceptual abstractions that help us understand (rather than experience) the world. While the notion of Zen is itself exceedingly useful in the quest for a better and more utilitarian interpretation of the world, it remains another product of the imagination: the idea of Zen, like all ideas, is entirely empty.

This is the meaning of Blyth's observation: no one understands Zen, in that understanding implies an intellectual exercise in which one abstraction is explained in terms of others. As Robert Heilbroner puts it,[2]

> By understanding I refer to the fact that we create conceptual order out of the plenum of stimuli that impinge from without and arise within. Perhaps it is more accurate to describe understanding as the manner in which we impose order on the plenum, creating unities and patterns of perception in a universe that reason tells us is only a "buzzing, blooming confusion."

We do not understand Zen for the obvious reason that Zen is precisely the absence of the attempt to "impose order" on our experience. By definition, to understand is to subject sensory data to an artificial conceptual framework. Given that Zen suggests the absence of the subjugation of experience to concepts, Zen is in effect the absence of understanding. Seen in this light, Zen itself is the final dualistic concept that must be abandoned in the name of mental hygiene. In much the same way that a successful student must ultimately give up her of his teachers, a true "understanding" of Zen ends (or, if you prefer, begins) with the rejection of Zen itself.

This in turn suggests a final paradox. Zen is (or rather, "is like") a state of consciousness in which the self, as conventionally understood, does not exist. Yet, because no one understands Zen, no one knows what it is, or, ultimately, how to find it. Instead, individuals discover Zen for themselves, rather than learning it from others. In this way, we are each authors of our own Zen, and thus, our own lives.

NOTES

1. Masao Abe, *Zen and Western Thought* (Honolulu: University of Hawaii Press, 1985), p. 6.
2. Robert Heilbroner, *The Nature and Logic of Capitalism*, (New York: W. W. Norton, 1985), p. 180.

INDEX

Abe, Masao: on consensus reality, 72; and Zen, 167; on *zazen*, 134

Abstractions: abandoned in Zen, 161; abstract thought, 26-27; defined, 11-12, 13n, 17, 18; good and evil, 159-162; methods of, 65; in politics, 160; purpose, 19, 22; versus reality, 27; relationship with science, 20. See also dualism

Amitabha, 130

anarchist theory: of nineteenth century, 147-152; Lao-tzu, 147; and liberty from social coercion, 149-151; and social institutions, 151

anatman. See *anatta*

anatta, 94

anicca, 94

anitya. See *anicca*

antimony, 24

Aristotle: on moderation, 93; principle of non-contradiction, 24; quote, 58

atman, 89-90; in Hinduism, 94

awakening, 101

awareness, 123; and *sesshin*, 125; and "one-pointedness," 129

Beats, 4

Beck, Charlotte Joko, 8

Blake, William, doors of perception, 32, 52

Blyth, R.H., 133, 166, 168

bodhi, 101. See also awakening

Bodhidharma, 101, 102; the wall, 105

bodhisattva, 96; Kwanzeon, 129

Bodhi Tree at Gaya, 91

Bosatsu. See *bodhisattva*

Brahman, 88; and *atman*, 89

bubble meditation. See meditation

Buddha, 91

Buddhism: and anarchists, 151-152; on birth and death, 95; and ego, 95; and enlightenment, 90; and Four Noble Truths, 91-92; and Hinduism, 93-95; on metaphysical/theological issues, 95; Pure Land, 130; relationship with Zen, 3; Sanskrit, 29; and *Upanishads*, 88; and *Veda*, 88

causality: defined, 24-25; understanding reality, 24

chanting. See meditation

Chao-Chao, 111

Chuang-tzu, 85; on dualism, 88

concepts: Cartesian coordinates, 29; conceptualize, 59; confusion over, 31; distinctions between reality, 39; dualistic concepts, 60; and ego, 41-42; practical significance, 39; to understand the universe, 31; understanding, 61

consensus reality, 70; arbitrariness, 66-67; ceases usefulness when, 73; ego, 72;

171

consensus reality (*continued*):
exited, 74; problem of life, 71;
subject-object division, 71-72

convention: and ego, 83; Lao-tzu
on, 83; social 82-83; as an abstraction, 154

darsana, 89

death, in Zen, 54

Descartes, 45; on a mechanistic
universe, 64; on self discovery, 77n

dhyana, 104. See also meditation

Dogen, 8

dualism, 19; and conventional
thinking, 28, 32; dualistic concepts, 60; good and evil, 158;
related to theories, 66; utility,
67. See also abstractions

dukkha, 90; in Four Noble
Truths, 92-93; in *Mahayana*,
96

ego, 40-41, 43; and boredom,
125; and chanting, 130; controlling, 51; ego-illusion, 41-43; and experience, 45-46;
and external world, 42; idea of
self, 44; and *koans*, 113; losing the ego, 49, 53-54; and
moksha, 90; seeing the ego,
47-48; spontaneity, 50; as a
tool, 54; view of reality, 41-42

Eightfold Path. See Noble Eightfold Path

Einstein: on gravity, 39; relationship with concepts, 23; Theory of Relativity, 23

enlightenment: American approach, 8; in Buddhism, 90;
establishment's notions, 7; experience and abstract from experience, 51-52; *satori*, 52;
and *Tao*, 97-98; Zen as a
method of liberation, 162-163.
See also spontaneous enlightenment

Fa-yen, 112

Four Noble Truths of Buddhism,
91

Freud: psychology of, 40; ego,
56n; on rules, 156

game theory, 67-68

Godel, Kurt: Godel's Theorum,
26, 73; and liar's paradox, 34n

Golas, Thaddeus, 2

Guatama, 91. See also Buddha

Huai-jang, 118

Heilbroner, Robert, 16, 168

Heisenberg's Uncertainty Principle, 24

Hekiganroku, 103

Hesse, Herman: on theories, 58;
on illusion, 38

hina. See *Mahayana*

Hinduism, versus Buddhism, 93-94

Hobbes: causation and determinism, 64; "law of the jungle,"
149

Hofstadter, Douglas, 34n

Hui-k'o, 103

Hui-neng, 104; on the mind, 105-106; and *satori*, 108; on *wu-wei*, 120

Hume, David, 34n; metaphysical
speculation, 76

Hung-jan, 104

Huxley, T.H., viii

Hsuan-tzu, 112

id, 40-41; differences from Zen,
43; goals of, 41-42

ideas, defined, 44

idealism (Berkeley), 34n

Jefferson, Thomas, on simplicity,
87

"Joshu's Mu," 111

Jung, Carl: on *satori*, 80; on
koan, 111

Kapleau, Philip, 13n

karma, 89; and *Nirvana*, 90; and
samsara, 90

Kasyapa. See *Mahakasyapa*

keisaku, 137

koan, 6, 109; toward enlightenment, 113-114; to exit consensus reality, 74; "Joshu's Mu,"
111-112; and *mondo*, 103-104; basic premise, 8-9, 110;
versus reason, 113; in Rinzai,
140-141; and *roshi*, 109; and
satori, 111; and self, 113;

Sakyamuni. See Buddha
salvation, 13n
samadhi, 93, 118; to experience reality, 121-122
samsara, 90; in *Mahayana*, 96
Sanskrit, 29; and *tathata*, 100
sanzen, 136
Sartre, 43
sat (real), 89
satori, 52, 56n, 80; and *koan*, 111; and meditation, 104-142. See enlightenment
Schopenhauer, Arthur, 16, 20; "id," 40
science, defined, 59
self. See ego
Seng-ts'an, 146
sesshin, 136-138
Shakespeare, William, viii
Shankara, 89
Shelley, Percy Bysshe, 87
Shen-hui, 106; on *samadhi*, 118
Siddhartha. See Buddha
smriti, 93
spontaneous enlightenment, 101
social coercion, 150-151
Soto, 107-108
Stalin, Joseph, 166
Sung period, 108
Sunyata, 98-100; and reality, 99; in *mondo*, 103
Suzuki, D.T., 4, 99; Essays in Zen Buddhism, 133; on *zazen*, 133-134
sutras, 129
symbolic systems, ix. See also language
tan, 136
T'ang period, 108
tanha, 92-93
Tantra, 129
Tao, 29; and dualistic thinking, 85; definition, 84; inconsistencies within, 97; and enlightenment, 87-88, 97-98; and pacificism, 115n; and *te*, 86. See also *wu-wei*
Tao-hsin, 104
taoism, 82; advent of, 82; and anarchy, 148; and convention,

82-83; as a system of thought, 84-85. See also *Tao*
Tao-sheng, spontaneous enlightenment, 101
Tao-te Ching, 82, 87
tat. See *tathata*
tathata, 29, 30, 100
te, 86; lesson of, 87; on ego and conventional thinking, 86; and Romantics or Transcendentalists, 87
"Ten-Clause Sutra," 129
thatness. See *tathata*
theory, 59-60, 64; anomalies of, 67, 69-70; Copernicus, 63; Crick and Watson on DNA, 62; game theory, 67-68; metatheory, 73-74; as models of reality, 62-63
Thoreau, Henry David, 87
Transcendental Meditation (TM), 129
Upanishads, 88
Veda, 88
Vedanta school, 89
Watts, Alan, 4; on decisions, 48-49; on dualistic arbitrary notions, 158; on *mondo*, 103; works of, 133
White, John, 38
Whitman, Walt, 87
Wienpahl, Paul, 127
Wittgenstein, Ludwig, 76
wu-wei, 85; and anarchy, 148; deviation from, 157; essence of, 109; and naturalness, 107, 120; and *smriti*, 93
yana. See *Mahayana*
yin-yang, 88
yoga, 52, 129
zazen, 7, 8; as an end, 133-134; method, 108-110; and monastic *sesshin*, 136; as *sesshin*, 124-125; simplicity of, 126; as a social activity, 124; techniques, 126-131. See also meditation
Zen, 32; abandoning abstractions, 161; abstruse nature discussion, 4, 5-7, 9;